PAUL

PASTOR OF COMMUNITIES FOR TODAY

Kevin J. Hanlon

PAUL

Pastor of communities
for today

St Paul Publications

Cover: St Paul at the Aeropagus by Raphael
        Reproduced by courtesy of the Board of Trustees of the
        Victoria and Albert Museum, London.

St Paul Publications
Middlegreen, Slough SL3 6BT, United Kingdom

Copyright © St Paul Publications UK 1991

ISBN 085439 365 X

Printed by The Guernsey Press Co. Ltd., Guernsey, C.I.

St Paul Publications is an activity of the priests and brothers of the Society of St Paul who proclaim the Gospel through the media of social communication

For Kathleen
in memory of our visit
to ancient Ephesus in 1989

Contents

Introduction   9

1. Aquila and Priscilla: lay people for our time   11
2. Corinth: a parish like ours today?   18
3. Paul: homeland missionary   24
4. Paul's doctor and Philippi   31
5. Paul and the Parousia   39
6. Paul's postcard to Philemon   47
7. Paul: faithful faith   53
8. Paul's vision of the Church   61
9. Christ and the Christian   69
10. Paul's pence for the poor   79
11. Paul's apologia   87
12. Pastor Paul (1)   95
13. Pastor Paul (2)   105
14. Paul and prayer   112

Appendices:

1. Paul: Time Chart   123
2. Paul: Letters   124
3. Missionary circle of Paul   125
4. Paul: Christian communities   127

Introduction

There are twenty-seven writings in the New Testament: four gospels, the Acts of the Apostles, twenty-one letters and the Book of Revelation. Of these letters fourteen are attributed to Paul. Across the centuries there has been doubt about Paul writing the letter to the Hebrews, and today it is generally not attributed to Paul. This still leaves virtually half the New Testament writings credited to Paul. It indicates the importance of the ex-persecutor convert in the life of the early Church, which is supported by half of the Acts of the Apostles devoted to the work of the Holy Spirit through him.

The hallmark of Paul's ministry is evangelisation and building up of Christian communities across the northern and eastern parts of the Mediterranean. In Greece and southern Turkey he was the founding father of several communities. In places like Damascus, Antioch in Syria, Ephesus and Rome he lived and worked with his fellow Christian pastors building up the young churches in Christ. He undertook correspondence with the communities he founded such as Corinth, Philippi and Thessalonica.

These communities – we would call them parishes today – lived in an affluent and permissive world akin to that of our time – a world alien to Christian values and the Christian life-style. Paul appreciated that they needed to be constantly built up in the Spirit if they were to withstand the pressures of such a society and to convert it to Christ. Paul carried out his role as pastor by visits, correspondence and sending delegates like Titus and Timothy, and also by establishing elders/presbyters to lead the communities in the Way of Christ.

The sheer force of Paul's faith and love for these young

communities shines through his letters and has ensured a place of importance in the New Testament canon. The letters work out the teaching of Jesus and the life in Christ in the Christian community. If Jesus preached and lived the Kingdom of God, his faithful disciple Paul left no stone unturned to bring Jesus Christ to the Jews and Gentiles of the Roman Empire; spared no effort to bring them into co-unity (community) in Christ. Paul saw Jew and Gentile in Christian fellowship as a miracle of God's power (Spirit) while the barrier of hatred between these two groups disappeared in Christ. As a previous hater himself (of Christians) Paul knew the difference between hate and the love of God in the Christian community. For Paul no hardship or suffering was too great to ensure the work of the Spirit in the building up of the emerging communities of Christ. Paul's testimony is as important for us today as it was in New Testament times. He stands as a pastor of communities for today.

1

Aquila and Priscilla:
lay people for our time

Every Christian has heard of St Paul, the apostle to the Gentiles – the pagans of the Roman Empire who lived in what we today call Europe (Italy, Greece, perhaps Spain) and Asia (Turkey, Syria, perhaps Jordan). Some Christians may recall Aquila and Prisca (short for Priscilla), missionary companions and co-workers of Paul, but take little notice of them. Many Christians would be surprised to know that Paul owed his life to this couple. Writing to the Christians in Rome, Paul first greets them:

> Greet Prisca and Aquila, my fellow workers in Christ Jesus, who risked their necks for my life, to whom not only I but also all churches of the Gentiles give thanks (Rom 16:3-4).

'Risking their necks' could mean that they held Roman citizenship, and in saving Paul's life risked the death penalty of beheading, which was the ultimate fate of Paul (he held Roman citizenship). Both Paul and the Gentile churches were grateful to this married Christian couple for saving Paul's life, and for the work in Christ they had done among the Gentiles and Gentile converts.

Luke tells us in the Acts of the Apostles that Paul first met this couple in Corinth. They had been expelled from Rome by an edict of the emperor Claudius. The Roman writer Suetonius gives us the reason for this expulsion in his book *The Twelve Caesars*:

> Because the Jews at Rome caused continuous disturbances at the instigation of Chrestus, Claudius expelled them from the city.

Luke, says Aquila, was a Jew so he may have been caught up in the continuous debate about Christ (Chrestus) which was rocking the synagogues in Rome. It is not clear from Luke whether or not this couple were already Christians when they arrived in Corinth about 49 AD, or were Paul's first converts in Corinth:

> He went to see them; and because he was of the same trade he stayed with them and they worked, for by trade they were tentmakers (Acts 18:2-3).

The Greek word for 'tentmakers' is *skenopoioi* which really means a leather worker. Cilicia, the area Paul came from, was famous for a fleece called *cilicium* made of goat's hair which was used for cloaks and hangings and was in great demand. If Paul was skilled in this leather work he would never have been out of work.

In those times shop and home were together, so Paul and his new friends lived and worked together in the same place. Their workshop was probably a centre of evangelisation since the Greeks used the workplace as an arena in which to philosophise (something akin to the French cafe in the recent past). Both the Acts and Paul's letters reveal a man who never lost an opportunity to speak about life in Christ whenever he had an audience, and the leather workshop provided Paul and his companions with a daily audience.

Luke relates that Aquila came from Pontus on the shores of the Black Sea, but tells us nothing about Priscilla. Aquila must have gone to Rome and carried out his trade in the imperial city. Perhaps it was in Rome that he had met and married Priscilla. William Barclay notes that in four out of the six references in the New Testament to this couple Prisca is named before her husband.[1] Normally the husband's name came first as we say and write 'Mr and Mrs'. Barclay conjectures that there is just a possibility that Prisca belonged to a noble Roman family and that Luke and Paul are indicating this when they put her name first. If she was a Gentile of noble birth then her marriage to the Jewish artisan, once they were converted, crossed the barriers of religion, sex and class spoken of by Paul to the Christians in Galatia:

> For as many of you as were baptised into Christ have put on Christ.
> There is neither Jew nor Greek,
> there is neither slave nor free,
> there is neither male nor female;
> for you are all one in Christ Jesus (Gal 3:27-28).

If Barclay's speculation is correct, this couple would have been a living symbol of what happens to those alive in Christ, i.e. joined for ever in Christian love and service with no divisive barriers. They would have been a living Christian symbol for both Jews and Gentiles coming together to live in Christian fellowship.

When Paul left Corinth and sailed to Ephesus, Prisca and Aquila went with him. Paul went on to Jerusalem, no doubt leaving his friends to set up shop and home in the cosmopolitan city. While Paul was away, a famous Jewish convert named Apollos from Alexandria in Egypt arrived in Ephesus. He was well versed in the Old Testament scriptures. Luke tells us that he had been instructed in the way of the Lord but knew only the baptism of John the Baptist (Acts 18:25-26), a point which illustrates the variety of ways people were coming into the Christian Church. When Aquila and Priscilla met him 'they took him and expounded to him the way of God more accurately' (Acts 18:26). The context of this story in the Acts indicates that

Apollos was then baptised in the name of the Lord Jesus and filled with the Holy Spirit by the laying on of hands. The Apollos story is dovetailed into Paul returning to Ephesus and meeting followers of the Baptist who are then baptised and confirmed in the Spirit (Acts 19:1-7), which is Luke's way of saying that the same happened to Apollos.

When Paul wrote from Ephesus to the Christians in Corinth he sent greetings from Aquila and Priscilla:

> The churches of Asia send greetings. Aquila and Prisca, together with the church in their house, send you hearty greetings in the Lord (1 Cor 16:19).

This greeting informs us that Paul's companions had a 'house-church' in Ephesus. They later had one in Rome, and Paul mentions it in his famous letter to the Christians in that city:

> Greet Prisca and Aquila ...
> greet also the church in their house (Rom 16:3, 5).

No doubt their work-house in Corinth was also a house-church. They were not alone in this pastoral scene. Another friend of Paul had a house-church in Colossae:

> To Philemon our beloved fellow worker and... the church in your house (Philem vv.1- 2).

The nearby town of Laodicea also:

> Give my greetings to the brethren at Laodicea, and to Nympha and the church in her house (Col 4:15).

At this time in the development of the Church there were no special buildings used for Christian worship. Up to the third century the Christians met in the houses of fellow Christians – Church and home were one and the same reality in Christ.

About 57 AD Paul left Ephesus and travelled to Corinth. Luke does not record Aquila and Prisca as journeying with him. From Corinth he is thought to have written his letter to the Christians in Rome in which he states his intention of visiting them at the centre of the empire. But first he was going to Jerusalem to take the collection of money from the churches of Asia for the saints who were poor in the Holy City. Then he would journey to Rome on his way to Spain (Rom 15:22). He greets Aquila and Prisca whom he knew to be back in the Eternal City.

Aquila and Priscilla are mentioned once more in the New Testament. Paul, writing probably from prison in Rome to Timothy in Ephesus, sends greetings to them:

Greet Prisca and Aquila ... (2 Tim 4:19).

Early on in the letter he reminded Timothy of the occasion when 'all who are in Asia turned away from me' (2 Tim 1:15). Asia here means the Roman province of Asia of which Ephesus was the capital city. If this statement refers to what happened in the past it could be an indirect reference to the riot in Ephesus described by Luke in Acts 19. Luke keeps Paul out of the riot and also out of Ephesus on his famous farewell journey to the churches of Asia in Acts (chapters 20 and 21). Luke must have had some reason for these omissions and one possibility is that Paul was imprisoned in Ephesus. Luke also makes no mention of the troubles Paul encountered with his fellow Christians in Corinth, and relates only one of Paul's three experiences of shipwreck, which we know about from Paul's correspondence with the Christians in Corinth (see 1 Cor 1:10-13 and 2 Cor 11:25). So it is possible that Luke omitted serious trouble for Paul in the capital of Asia just as he did not relate Paul's execution in Rome.[2] Very serious trouble for Paul in Ephesus would have given Aquila and Priscilla the opportunity to risk their lives in order to save him from the Roman authorities when all other Christians had abandoned him.

Paul himself makes two statements in the Corinthian letters which tell us of serious trouble in the province of Asia and its capital Ephesus:

> In Asia... we despaired of life itself... we felt we had received the sentence of death... God... delivered us from so deadly a peril (2 Cor 1:8-10).
> I fought with beasts at Ephesus (1 Cor 15:32).

The last quotation is usually interpreted metaphorically. If taken literally this could have been the occasion on which Aquila and Priscilla risked their lives to save him since no Roman citizen could be cast to the beasts.

What can we learn from these few snapshots of Aquila and Priscilla in the New Testament? The snaps are there for a purpose. They reveal a husband and wife as co-workers of the apostle Paul with house-churches in their homes in Rome, Corinth and Ephesus. Their houses were also their workplaces and probably centres of evangelisation in regard to their neighbours and customers. They were always spoken of together in both Acts and Paul's letters. If in their marriage they had crossed the sexist, religious and socio-political barriers of their time, then they were a powerful sign of life in Christ, not just to the pagans but also to Christian communities around the empire. In our time Pope John Paul II at York (1982) called marriage a ministry:

> Christian marriage is a sacrament of salvation.
> Yours is a true and proper ministry in the Church.

In his letter *The Christian Family in the Modern World* (1981) he calls the Christian family the 'domestic church'. Married Christians today are being called in the spirit of Aquila and Priscilla to be sacramental signs to our times, to be witnesses to life in the Spirit of the risen Christ.

Christians are being called to see their marriage and family life as a missionary domestic church to a world in darkness and in need of the light of Christ. Aquila and Priscilla are an example to inspire us. They were co-workers with their pastor (Paul). Their home was a centre of Church life. Their home-shop, their workplace, was a centre of evangelisation for Christ. They were prepared to lay down their lives for their pastor. There can be no sign of greater love, Jesus said, than to lay down one's life for a friend.

NOTES

[1] There are three references in Acts and three in Paul's letters to Aquila and Priscilla: Prisca and Aquila (2 Tim 4:19); Prisca and Aquila (Acts 18:18); Prisca and Aquila (Rom 16:3); Priscilla and Aquila (Acts 18:26); Aquila and Priscilla (2 Cor 16:19); Aquila and Priscilla (Acts 18:2).

[2] Luke was probably writing in the 80s AD, when Roman authorities had begun to persecute the Christians in various places. In writing the Acts of the Apostles Luke showed that in the early days of the Church Roman authority tolerated Christianity and it was not seen as a threat to the empire.

2

Corinth:
a parish like ours today?

In looking back to former times there is always the danger of over-romanticising the past: childhood days seem idyllic, late teens and early twenties appear as the special years, and in the same way, the parishes of the past seem to be centres of spiritual security and stability.

The early Church of New Testament times is often seen as something of a golden age. This is partly due to St Luke, who wrote the Acts of the Apostles with a touch of the epic style. His two central apostles, Peter and Paul, stride across the stage of the Roman Empire, preaching the Gospel with missionary boldness, and converts come into the Church in leaps and bounds: 120 (Acts 1:15), then 3,000 (Acts 2:41), and finally 'converts multiplied greatly' (Acts 6:7).

When we turn to the letters of the New Testament, though, a different view is opened up for us. The Church had its problems: how were slaves and free people to relate in the Christian community? Were Gentiles to become Jews first, undergoing circumcision before becoming Christians? How were Jewish converts, who had scrupulously kept apart from pagans, to sit in Eucharistic table fellowship with their Gentile converts? How were Christians to live in a permissive empire and convert it to Christ?

These 'barrier issues' were not easy to solve. And they are still with us in a different form in our own times, for example, born Catholics relating to converts; coming together with our separated brethren; class consciousness in our churches; and coping with a permissive society to survive as Christians, let alone converting it!

From the fourth century onwards, the word 'parish' (from the Latin *parochia*) and 'diocese' were used side by side to mean an area under a bishop. In fact, 'parish' and 'diocese' were synonymous until the Middle Ages. The distinction between a diocese, which was under a bishop, and a parish, under a parish priest, was established at the beginning of the Middle Ages, and has come down as such in our times. In the New Testament writings, the word *ecclesia* (assembly) was used to describe the Church at a universal level (Eph 1:22), regional level (1 Cor 16:1) and local level (1 Cor 1:2). The use of *ecclesia* went further and was applied to the house-churches of the Christians around the empire: Aquila and Priscilla sent greetings from the church in their house at Ephesus to the Christians in Corinth (1 Cor 16:17), and Paul, writing from Corinth to Rome, sent greetings to this couple in Rome and the church in their house (Rom 16:3-5). From the three letters of John in the New Testament, we can detect a circle of house-churches as the basis of the Johannine Church community. So, from the evidence we possess, it seems that the 'Church' of the New Testament comprised circles of house-churches in a city or town, or a wider area which in later ages would become diocese and parish.

Paul's contact with Corinth (*the* vice city of the Roman world) reveals a missionary pastor seeking to be a shepherd to his newly-converted 'fledgeling flock'. According to Luke, Paul arrived in the city on his second missionary journey, about the winter of 50 AD, and stayed for eighteen months (Acts 18:11). Luke mentions another visit on the third missionary journey, about 57 AD, when Paul stayed in

Corinth for about three months (Acts 20:3). But we know from Paul's correspondence that he made another visit between the two mentioned by Luke: 'I am ready to come to you for the third time' (2 Cor 12:14). This visit is called the 'painful visit' because it caused distress for Paul (2 Cor 2:1-4).

Cliques and problems

When Paul left Corinth after his first visit, it appears that a variety of problems arose in this charismatic community. Members of Chloe's household (a house-church) went to Ephesus to inform Paul about the problems the community faced. Some Christians had become filled with their own importance and were causing the community to break into factious cliques:

I belong to Paul,
I belong to Apollos,
I belong to Cephas (Peter),
I belong to Christ (1 Cor 1:12).

Paul was appalled. Nine times in the opening nine verses of 1 Corinthians he mentions Christ and asks, 'Is Christ divided?' Paul knew that such divisions would eventually destroy the local Christian community.

Each of the cliques was focusing on a key figure to support their own views of Christianity. Peter was probably being looked to by the Jewish Christians wishing to keep Jewish traditions. Apollos was an eloquent orator from Alexandria in Egypt, looked to by the free and educated Gentile Christians in the city. Paul, apostle to the Gentiles, preaching Christ crucified, would appeal to the converted slaves. The Christ group may have been stressing that they were the true followers of Christ.

Paul approves of none of the cliques. He concentrates on getting the Christian life-style in perspective:

I did not come proclaiming to you the testimony of God in lofty words or wisdom (1 Cor 2:1).
We preach Christ crucified... (1 Cor 1:23).
I appeal to you, brethren, by the name of Our Lord Jesus Christ, that all of you agree and that there be no dissensions among you, but that you be united in the same mind and the same judgement (1 Cor 1:10).

The arrogant spirit which was at work in some of the Christians in Corinth was leading to a whole series of interrelated problems:

- they were taking each other to civil courts (1 Cor 6:1-11);
- some were supporting incestuous type of marriage (1 Cor 5);
- others were fornicating and justifying such conduct (1 Cor 6:12-20);
- the strong (mature) Christians were eating sacrificial meat from pagan temples, sold off in the marketplace, regardless of how this offended the 'weaker' Christians (1 Cor 8 and 10);
- even the Eucharist was being abused by people getting drunk and over-eating at the agape buffet which seems to have preceded the Eucharistic celebration (1 Cor 11:17-33).

Paul's instructions on these issues were that if they were hungry and thirsty, they should eat and drink in their own homes, which implies that they met in centralised houses for the Eucharist. They could eat meat sacrificed to idols, but not if it would scandalise outsiders or those with sensitive consciences. Their bodies should be for the glory of God since they were temples of the Holy Spirit. The man living in an unacceptable marriage relationship should be excommunicated. And rather than taking each other to court they should settle their differences together, and even suffer a wrong in the spirit of Christ.

The need for love

Paul acknowledged the giftedness of the Corinthian Christians in the Spirit (1 Cor 1:4). In chapter 12 of 1 Corinthians, he lists their gifts and links them with ministries and services within, and for, the local Christian community. But in his famous passage on love in chapter 13, he states that all gifts and services are pointless unless they are rooted in Christian love – 'make love your aim' (14:1). His final greeting is based on love: 'my love be with you all in Christ Jesus' (16:24).

The gifts of healing and tongues, prevalent in Corinth, have emerged in our time through the charismatic movement. The gift of tongues, in particular, has its controversial side, as it did in Corinth. Paul devoted chapters 12 and 14 of 1 Corinthians to getting the gifts of tongues and prophecy in perspective. In his lists of gifts and ministries, Paul puts tongues last. He did not forbid speaking or singing in tongues (he was a speaker in tongues himself) but suggests a pattern of liturgy with a place and procedure for tongues (1 Cor 12:26-35).

Women's role in the liturgy also features in 1 Corinthians. Women were both praying and prophesying at liturgical gatherings. (In fact, the early Church had prophetesses: see Acts 21:9.) In chapter 11, the issue is not whether or not they should do, but whether they should wear a head-covering when they prayed and prophesied in the liturgy. Head wear for women was an issue for us some decades ago, and likewise in Corinth. Presumably, the Jewish Christian women were wearing veils, while the more liberated free Gentile Christian women were not covering their heads. This was a source of controversy within the community. Paul needed the wisdom of Solomon on the issue. He does not impose a solution but pointed out the practice of the churches of God, which was for women to have their heads covered.

At the heart of 1 Corinthians is Paul's famous hymn on Christian love. Without the love which Christ radiates, the life of the community is meaningless. It was this spirit of love that was lacking among the Corinthian Christians, and was the root cause of their problems. One could give away everything to the poor, be a martyr, but if these actions are not inspired by Christian love, they count for nothing (13:3) – they are done for self-glory and not the glory of God in Christ.

In Paul's lists of gifts of the Spirit (1 Cor 12; Rom 12:6-8; Eph 4:11-12; Gal 5:22-24), love, peace and joy emerge as the three key gifts of life in Christ, both individually and in community. According to Luke it was the gift of Christian love which enabled the saints in Jerusalem to sell their property and share their goods and food gladly and generously (Acts 2:46). They also had the Spirit of peace, which is crucial for community life in Christ: 'The whole group of believers were united in heart and soul (Acts 4:32). It was a community looked up to by everyone, and a source of converts (Acts 2:47).

With the re-emergence of the role of the laity in our time, highlighted by Pope John Paul II's letter *Christifideles Laici* (The Lay Faithful) in 1989, Paul's first letter to the Corinthians deserves to be studied by every parish. It is the writing in the New Testament that gives us a window into a local Church community (parish), twenty years on from the time of Jesus. It can inspire, and remind, us to make love our aim in the use of the gifts of the Spirit in Christ's body as missionaries for today.

3

Paul: homeland missionary

The Letter to the Galatians

Many people probably think that St Paul spent most of his missionary life away from his home in Tarsus and his country, which we today know as Turkey. On reading the Acts of the Apostles, we see him in Judaea, Syria, Arabia, Cyprus, Greece, Rome and perhaps visiting Spain (see Rom 15). On analysis, however, Paul actually spent the longest period of missionary work in his homeland of Turkey. Luke records three years in Ephesus (Acts 20:30), and each of the three missionary journeys in Acts features Paul at work in other parts of Turkey:

First Journey: About 45 AD, Paul and Barnabas evangelised in the south Galatian cities of Antioch, Iconium, Lystra and Derbe.

Second Journey: About 49 AD, Paul and Silas (Silvanus) went via Cilicia (Paul's home province) to the South Galatian cities. At Lystra, Timothy joined them and they travelled through North Galatia to Troas.

Third Journey: Paul travelled from Antioch in Syria (his missionary base) via Cilicia to Ephesus, encouraging the Christians in the Galatian churches. When he left Ephesus he journeyed to Corinth, but hugged the Turkish coast on his voyage back to Jerusalem, stopping at Troas, Assos, Mitylene, Miletus and Patara.

After possible release from house arrest in Rome about 62 AD, Paul may have visited Ephesus again (1 Tim 1:3) before his eventual martyrdom in Rome in the mid-sixties AD.

The three years in Ephesus, religious capital of Asia, marked an outbreak of correspondence for Paul with nearby young Christian churches:

Letters from Ephesus	Addressed to	Our designation
a. to parts of Turkey	Colossae	Colossians
	Laodicea	(letter lost)
	Galatian churches	Galatians
	Philemon	Philemon
b. to Greece	Philippi (?)	Philippians
	Corinth	1 & 2 Corinthians

Paul was a Jewish 'Turk' with Roman citizenship (Acts 16:37), speaking Greek, Aramaic and Hebrew. In his letter to the converts of Galatia, perhaps written during his last sojourn in Ephesus or Corinth, he speaks to his own people and does not hesitate to call them 'foolish':

O foolish Galatians! Who has bewitched you, before whose eyes Jesus Christ was publicly portrayed as crucified? (3:1).

I am astonished that you are so quickly deserting him who called you in the grace of Christ and turning to a different gospel (1:6).

Before tackling this problem Paul devotes the first section of the letter to his own personal history (1:11-2:10). He admits that he had persecuted the Church and tried to destroy it. Luke fills this out in more detail in the Acts of the Apostles, showing Paul's part in the stoning of Stephen (Acts 7:58), Paul breathing threats and murder against men and women disciples (9:1-2), hunting them down and putting them in prison (22:3-5), and torturing them in synagogues by flogging to make them deny Christ (26:11). After his conversion Paul was to receive a taste of his own medicine since he received the thirty-nine lashes in synagogues five times (2 Cor 11:24).

Thin end of the wedge

Paul relates his call by God's grace to reveal Christ to the pagans (the Gentiles), and he stresses that the Gospel came through a revelation of Jesus Christ, points that Luke depicts in the famous Damascus Road story in Acts 9. Luke tells us that Paul was temporarily blinded at his conversion, and had to be led into Damascus. Paul tells us that he went to Arabia and later *returned* to Damascus (Gal 2:17), which implies that he had been in Damascus as Luke relates. He also gives us a brief résumé of his itinerary after his conversion:

> I went away into Arabia [modern Jordan] (1:17). Then after three years I went up to Jerusalem to visit Cephas (1:18), then I went into the regions of Syria and Cilicia (1:21), then after fourteen years I went up again to Jerusalem... (2:1) and... met Cephas (2:9).

Dovetailed with this chronology are three crucial missionary statements:

> – When he [God] had called me through his grace... that I might preach him among the Gentiles... (1:15-16);
> – When they perceived the grace given to me, James and Cephas and John... gave to me the right hand of fellowship, that we should go to the Gentiles... (2:29);
> – When Cephas came to Antioch [after Paul's second visit to Jerusalem] I opposed him... [he would not eat with Gentiles] (2:11).

Behind all these statements, Paul is defending his call by God to be an apostle and to be approved in the ministry by the Mother Church in Jerusalem and by Peter (Cephas, the Rock). The implication is that opponents of Paul's preaching and teaching had visited the churches in Galatia and disturbed them about Paul's status in the Church with accusations that he was not a genuine apostle, but a self-styled ex-persecutor and upstart.[1] These opponents were probably strict Jewish converts who believed God's Law of the Old Testament should be fully observed. They saw Paul's preaching of freedom in Christ, with no need for circumcision for Gentile converts, as the thin end of the wedge for the disappearance of observance of God's Law. They probably pointed to Cephas as having changed his mind about too much openness to the Gentile converts. Paul tells us that Cephas did eat with Gentile converts (i.e. sit down to Eucharistic table fellowship with them) in Antioch in Syria until Christian members of the circumcision party came from Jerusalem to bring about a change of policy (Gal 2:11-13). So effective was their propaganda that Cephas, the rest of the Jewish converts, and even Barnabas, stopped him sitting in table fellowship with Gentile converts (Gal 2:12-13).

Crucial issue

Fear must have been behind the 'back-down'; fear that the circumcision party had a very real point; fear that the cherished Law of God would eventually be cast aside by the wedge of 'no circumcision'; fear that increasing numbers of Gentile converts would swamp the Jewish Christians; fear of changing the habits of a lifetime and regarding the despised and unclean Gentiles as brothers and sisters in Christ. Paul saw the 'heart of the matter' and what was really at stake in this issue. If the circumcision party (the Judaisers) won the day, Christianity would end up as a sect and not a faith for all nations. He had to stand up to Peter in front of a gathering of the Jewish Christians and tell him he was wrong. Peter's example and leadership was crucial.

Peer stood condemned; he feared the circumcision party and acted insincerely, and was not straightforward about the truth of the Gospel.

We are not told whether Peter and the Jewish Christians changed their stance after hearing Paul out. Paul seems to have stood out alone on this issue. For him it was crucial, and he challenged Peter, presenting the truth that in Christ there is neither Jew nor Gentile, and all are one (Gal 3:28). Paul hoped that Cephas would be true to this truth of the Gospel freedom in Christ.

The conflict with Peter and the bewitching of the Galatians was rooted in the fundamental problem of justification – how do sinful men and women get into a right relationship with God (righteousness)? Is it:

a. by carrying out the works of God's Law given in the Old Testament, which Jesus came not to abolish but to fulfil?

b. by faith in Christ?

This question reverberated again at the Reformation, leading to the Reformers' slogan of 'justification by faith alone'. The correct formula is 'justification by grace through faith'.

Freedom

In chapters 3 and 4 of Galatians, Paul works out the difference between what can be called 'Law-based righteousness' and 'faith righteousness'. He focusses on Abraham, founding father of Judaism, who was a man of faith and in a right relationship with God 430 years before the Law was given to Moses (Gal 3:6-17). When the Law was given, it was a pedagogue until Christ came (3:24). The word 'pedagogue' (trainer) referred to a male servant who looked after a young boy, rather like a male nanny, until he came of age at 16. So for Paul, the Law was for a period of human adolescence, showing the need for Christ

28

and the spiritual adulthood he lived out and empowers all to receive by faith.

For Paul, it is impossible to achieve a right relationship with God by one's own efforts, which is a view the Law produces. Even those who were circumcised did not keep the Law (6:13). Paul himself had tried more than others to advance in Judaism beyond his peers (1:14) in this quest of being right with God. As a devout follower of the Law, he had ended up as a killer of Christians! The ineffectiveness of trying to keep the Law by one's own efforts is mapped out by Paul in Romans 7:14-25 with his cry of 'wretched man that I am! Who will deliver me? Thanks be to God... Jesus Christ'.

All attempts at Law-based righteousness, for Paul, led to slavery. Obsession with one's own righteousness, which Law-based righteousness produces, leads to life in the flesh instead of life in the Spirit (Gal 3:1-5). In chapter 5 he vividly contrasts the two life-styles in list form, which was a common practice at that time:

– fifteen works of life in the flesh (e.g. strife, anger, partisan spirit) are listed in Galatians 5:19-21;

– nine fruits of life in the Spirit (e.g. love, joy, peace) are given in 5:22-23.

Chapters 5:1 to 6:10 could be entitled 'freedom from slavery of sin (life in the flesh) through life in the Spirit'. There are nine references to the Spirit and three to freedom. Christ has called us to freedom, and for freedom Christ has set us free. This freedom is *from* the slavery of sin, mapped out in his catalogue of life in the flesh (see Rom 1:24-32), and freedom *for* life in the Spirit of the risen Christ, i.e. service to others, bearing one another's burdens (6:2).

The theme of freedom reaches its peak halfway through the letter in the profound insight that in Christ 'there is no Jew or Greek, there is neither slave nor free, there is neither male nor female; you are all one in Christ' (3:28).

We still have to live out and fulfil this in-depth perspective of life in the Spirit in which the three terrible barriers of human relationships are overcome in Christ –

the religious barrier (Jew and Gentile), the socio-political barrier (slave and free person), and the sexist barrier (male and female).

Paul saw clearly that these barriers, which mar human life and relationship, can only be overcome when men and women are in a right relationship with God. Only the Power (Spirit) of God can overcome such apparently insurmountable barriers, which we have seen so glaringly in the twentieth century. It is through humility of faith in the Spirit that the hope of righteousness lies (5:5). Paul's advice to his bewitched homeland fellow-Christians, and to us in our bewitched times, is:

Walk by the Spirit
Live by the Spirit
Be led by the Spirit, for
'he who sows to the Spirit will from the Spirit reap eternal life' (6:8).

NOTE

[1] If to others I am not an apostle, at least I am to you; for you are the seal of my apostleship in the Lord (1 Cor 9:2).

4

Paul's doctor and Philippi

The Letter to the Philippians

In the Acts of the Apostles (16:11), Luke records that St Paul sailed from Troas (north-west Turkey) to Neapolis, the port for Philippi (in north-east Greece), which is described as the 'first city' of Macedonia. Philippi was a veteran Roman soldier colony. The retired soldiers were a strategic 'territorial army/home guard', easily mobilised in time of military need. It was, therefore, a city with a definite form of Roman law and administration – a miniature version of Rome itself. Thessalonica, further south, was the provincial capital, so 'first city' was an honorary title indicating Philippi's importance.

Paul's crossing from Asia to Europe is given special significance. Luke related that in Troas, Paul had a dream of a 'man of Macedonia' calling him over into Europe. It has been suggested that his vision-man was Alexander the Great. Troas' full name was 'Alexandrian Troas', and Thessalonica was named after Alexander's half-sister, and Philippi after his father, Philip of Macedon. Alexander's great dream was to marry East and West (Asia and Europe), making one world.[1] Perhaps Paul's vision was focussed on Alexander's dream, but rooted in making one world for Christ.

The beloved physician

Another suggestion is that perhaps Luke himself was the Macedonian man who was inspirational in getting Paul to cross into Europe, and that Philippi was Luke's home or place of work. From this point in Acts, a series of passages in which 'they' is replaced by 'we' begins (16:10-17; 20:5-15; 21:1-8; 27:1-28:16). The first passage moves from Troas to Philippi (on Paul's second journey), and stops there, then resuming at 20:5 (third journey) when Paul crossed back from Philippi to Troas, sailing from Jerusalem to Rome where he was placed under house arrest. The precise details contained in these 'we' passages indicate a travel log or journal which was later used in Acts. The pivotal role of Philippi has led to a view that Luke met Paul in Troas and invited him to visit this Roman colony.

The New Testament makes only three statements about Luke, and these are all by Paul:

> Luke the beloved physician... (Col 4:14);
> Luke, my fellow worker... (Philem v. 24);
> Luke alone is with me... (2 Tim 4:11).

Later writers fill in more details about Luke and his relationship with Paul: the Muratorian Canon (c. 170 AD) says Paul took Luke along with him. Tertullian (c. 160-240 AD) called Paul Luke's inspirer. Irenaeus (end of 2nd century) says Luke was the inseparable companion of Paul. A second-century prologue to Luke's gospel states that Luke was a follower of Paul, that he was a Syrian of Antioch without wife or children, and died aged 84 in Boetia (Greece) full of the Holy Spirit.[2]

Luke records two conversion stories in Philippi through the missionary work of Paul, Silas, Timothy and Luke (if he is included in the 'we' passages):

1. A Jewish business woman called Lydia, who was baptised with all her household.

2. The Gentile city jailer and his family.

Luke emphasises the community aspect of conversion, something that he also does in Acts, especially in relation to the household of the centurion Cornelius (Acts 10:2,

28, 48). The Church of New Testament times was a 'domestic church'.

Paul and Silas were instrumental in converting the jailer and his family because they had been beaten and imprisoned for exorcising a soothsaying girl, who was a slave, and a slave to her owner's greed. They were profiteering by exploiting her spirit of divination. The symbol of soothsaying in the Graeco-Roman world was the python at Delphi. Women soothsayers were known as 'pythos'. Paul exorcised her alien spirit in the name of Jesus Christ. For this act of Christian healing, he and Silas had to endure the fury of her deprived owners, beating with rods, and the overnight torture of a zulon – an excruciating form of stocks inside the prison cell. Yet Luke says that they were 'praying and singing hymns to God' during the night (Acts 16:25). It is interesting to note that in the calm of the following morning, Paul appeals to the Roman citizenship, which puts fear into the magistrates in Roman Philippi. It is likely that most of the Christian converts were Roman citizens in this colony with its exceptional civic privileges.

Special relationship

Paul does not appear to have stayed long in Philippi. He made two further visits on his third missionary journey, and wrote a letter from prison to them, perhaps from Ephesus about 57 AD, which would recall both to Paul and his beloved Philippians his incarceration in their city jail several years before.

Philippians 3:1 hints that Paul had written to them previously, and a close examination of the letter suggests a compilation of three letters edited into our epistle to the Christians in Philippi. The Letter to the Philippians in the New Testament canon radiates joy, recalling the singing in jail recorded by Luke in Acts. There is the joy that Christ is preached (1:18), the joy of faith (1:25), the joy of prayer

(1:4), the joy of suffering for Christ (2:17), the joy of Christian hospitality (2:29), the joy of conversion (4:1), and joy as a gift (4:1). Paul even calls the Christian community at Philippi 'my joy and my crown' (4:1). This designation reflects Paul's special relationship with the Philippian Christians. Even the tone of the letter is more personal than any other of his letters.

The Philippian Christian community was the one that never gave Paul any trouble. It was the only one he allowed to assist him financially – twice they sent aid to him in Thessalonica (Phil 4:16), once to Corinth (2 Cor 11:9), and again via Epaphroditus when he wrote the letter from prison (Phil 4:18). There must have been some special reason why Paul permitted this help from Philippi and from no other Christian community. One reason might be that no other local church in his early missionary days wanted too much liaison with this ex-persecutor (Phil 3:6) except the Philippian community (Phil 4:15). Another could be that his companion doctor had roots in Philippi. Paul supported himself by his craft as a leather-worker (Acts 18:3; 1 Cor 9:6), but he may not have been able to meet the 'medical expenses' owed to Luke.

Appeal for unity

It makes sense that Paul needed the help of a physician to undertake the strenuous and demanding missionary activity recorded in Acts. Those who have added up the miles Paul covered by road and ship wonder how on earth he travelled such distances. It was a daunting task for a healthy man, never mind the 'wreck' Paul must have been after his sufferings for Christ: five times flogged in syna-gogues, three beatings with rods, stoned once (and left for dead – Acts 14:19), three shipwrecks, in continuous danger from brigands, sleepless nights, hungry and thirsty, cold and lacking clothing (see 2 Cor 11:24). There was also a 'thorn in the flesh' (2 Cor 12:7).

To keep me from being too elated... a thorn was given me in the flesh... to harass me... Three times I besought the Lord... that it should leave me, but he said to me, 'My grace is sufficient for you, for my power is made perfect in weakness.' (2 Cor 12:7-9).

In the Old Testament, thorn refers to enemies. So Paul's thorn in the flesh may have been the enemies who constantly hounded him across his missionary years (Jews and even Jewish fellow Christians). Paul saw 'internal opposition' whether among his own people, or fellow Christians, as a great hindrance to the work of God in Christ (1 Cor 1:10).

Writing to the Christians in Galatia, Paul refers to a bodily ailment, and this was the reason why he left the coastland of southern Turkey and moved up to evangelise them on the higher plateau land (Gal 4:13). This would make sense if Paul suffered from malaria, which could devastate the coastal areas of Turkey in Paul's time. Malaria fits in with Paul's description of his ailment: 'And though my condition was a trial to you, you did not scorn or despise me' (Gal 4:14). Here we have another possible reason why later on Paul would need the medical services of a doctor.

Some people find the letter to Philippi the most attractive of Paul's letters. It has been described as a friendly letter to his converts, relating news about himself and their goodwill representative, Epaphroditus, warning against the evil workmen (3:2) who are ruining his work in Christ in other places and who might arrive in Philippi, and, above all, appealing for unity in the Christian community. The workers of evil may have been the Judaisers, i.e. those seeking to impose the Law of Moses and circumcision on the Gentile converts. Paul's feelings about them burst forth in three warnings:

1. 'Look out for dogs.' Here Paul was saying that in their proud self-righteousness, the Judaisers called the Gentiles 'dogs', but in fact it is they who are the dogs because they pervert the Gospel.

2. 'Look out for the evil workers.' They were sure that by keeping the Law they were working good, but for Paul they were really working evil. By imposing a life-style of self-righteousness, they were alien to God's righteousness in Christ.

3. 'Look out for those who mutilate the flesh.' They gloried in the outward sign of circumcision of the flesh, but in their inner hearts and minds, they were self-mutilated (see Phil 3:2-3).

The main pastoral points of the letter to Philippi focus on:

Fight for the faith (2:27-30). Their lives must be worthy of the Gospel. They must stand firm and not be afraid of opponents.

Here is one of several Roman military images which Paul uses for the Christians in this Roman military colony. Stand firm (*stekete*) was an order given to a soldier in the thick of battle. In 4:7 he says the peace of God will guard (*phrourein*) your hearts. *Phrourein* was a military term for standing guard. Epaphroditus is a fellow-soldier (2:25). To a colony proud of its Roman citizenship, he says that our citizenship is in heaven (3:20). He opens and closes the letter with a reference to Caesar. The Gospel has become known throughout the praetorian guard (Caesar's special army) where Paul is imprisoned, and there are even converts among Caesar's household where Paul is being held (4:21).

Work for salvation (2:12-18). God is at work in them, so be blameless and innocent children of God in a crooked and perverse generation, shining as lights in the world. The word Paul uses for 'lights' is the same as that used in the Greek version of the Old Testament in Genesis 1 for the lights God set in the firmament of heaven, i.e. the sun and the moon. In Genesis, the sun and moon rule the day and night. Paul sees the Christians as having a similar task in the darkness which constitutes the world of people (see Rom 1:18-32).

Follow the way of salvation (3:2-4:1). Against the Judaisers, Paul asserts, 'We [Christians] are the true circumcision, who worship God in spirit, and glory in Christ Jesus, and put no confidence in the flesh' (3:3). We are put into a right relationship with God ('righteousness') through faith in Christ and the power of Christ's resurrection, in which we share. We don't get into a right relationship with God through our own efforts. Paul asks them to be mature-minded and imitate him. For any Christian to ask his or her fellow Christian to imitate them is a bold challenge. Paul could challenge them in this way because he had suffered so much in Christ that he was closely identified with him. Paul had a deep experience of being 'in Christ', a phrase he probably coined. It is from deep suffering in Christ and from imprisonment that he can challenge them to imitate him as he imitated Christ. He also warns them against those who are enemies of the cross (sufferings) of Christ. Stand firm against them (4:1).

Community in humility is a central theme of this letter. In 4:2-3, he entreats two women, Euodia and Syntyche, who have been fellow-workers of Paul, to cease their dispute and agree in Christ. He follows this appeal with an exhortation to rejoice, pray and be at peace (4:4-7). Peace also appears in the opening greeting of the letter. The Greek word *eirene* translated the Hebrew *shalom*, which means 'make peace'. Peace is an activity of the Spirit in the Christian. We are to be peace-makers, we are to weave peace like a web in which to catch people.

The whole basis of any Christian community in humility is rooted into what the Father has done in Christ, which Paul expresses in an early Christian hymn in 2:6-11. Here is the model for every Christian in community with Christ. It is probably the greatest and most moving passage Paul ever used concerning Jesus.[3] This hymn may have been familiar to Paul's doctor, since he included several hymns and canticles in his famous infancy narrative.

Have this mind among yourselves in Christ Jesus,
Who, being in the form of God
did not consider it a prize

to be equal with God
but emptied himself
taking the form of a slave.
Having become in the likeness of men
and being found in shape as a man
he humbled himself
becoming obedient unto death.
Therefore, God super-exalted him
and gave him the Name
which is above all names
so that at the name of Jesus
every knee should bow
and every voice proclaim
'The Lord is Jesus Christ.'[4]

NOTES

[1] This is a vision which Pope John Paul II has in our time, especially of the re-united world of Roman and Orthodox Christianity.

[2] There is nothing to prevent Luke's home being in Antioch in Syria, and his medical career centred in Philippi. The period of the Roman Empire was one of the great ages of travel.

[3] There are three main possibilities about this hymn:
  a. It was composed by Paul;
  b. Paul used an existing hymn;
  c. An existing hymn was inserted by an editor.

[4] This translation is taken from *Paul* by L. Wright, second edition, Sheed & Ward, 1971.

5

Paul and the Parousia

Luke relates Paul, Timothy and Silas (Silvanus) arriving in Thessalonica from Philippi on Paul's second missionary journey about 50 AD. Paul and Silas had been flogged and imprisoned in Philippi which Paul mentions in his first letter to Thessalonica (2:2). This was the first of three visits to the city named after Alexander the Great's half-sister. The other two visits were made on the third missionary journey.

Thessalonica ranked next to Athens in ancient Greece. It was the capital of the province of Macedonia. Here Paul and his missionary companions stayed at the house of Jason. Paul spent three weeks arguing with the Jews of the synagogue that it was necessary for the expected Messiah (in Greek 'Christ') to suffer and rise from the dead. Some Jews were converted and a great many devout Greeks (Acts 17:4). The majority of converts coming from paganism is reflected in the first letter to Thessalonica:

What a welcome we had among you,
and how you turned to God from idols,
to serve a living and true God (1:9).

The 'flip' side of this welcome was a riot organised by the Jews. A mob attacked Jason's house searching for Paul and Silas, who were both Jewish Christians (Timothy had a Greek father and Jewish mother). Thwarted in their purpose they dragged Jason and some other Christians before the city politarchs (non-Roman magistrates) and used the same propaganda as had been used against Jesus in Jerusalem:

They are all acting against the decrees of Caesar, saying that there is another king, Jesus (Acts 17:7; see Jn 19:12, Lk 23:2).

This accusation disturbed the city authorities. The Christians decided to get Paul and Silas out of Thessalonica sending them by night south to Beroea. But even here Paul was not safe. When the Jews of Thessalonica heard that many Jews and even more Gentiles were being converted they went to Beroea and incited mob trouble again. Paul had to leave Timothy and Silas, and take ship to Athens (Acts 17:10-15).

It appears from the first letter to Thessalonica (3:1-2) that Timothy joined Paul in Athens and was then sent back to Thessalonica to help build the Christians up in faith in a setting of continuing persecution. Paul anxiously waited for news. When he could wait no longer 'I sent [possibly Silas] that I might know your faith,' i.e. know how they were getting on (1 Thess 3:5).

Corinth was the city from which Paul undertook his correspondence with Thessalonica – the letters known as 1 and 2 Thessalonians. The two letters are slightly different in length but similar in structure and content. Both are sent out in the names of the missionary team – Paul, Silas and Timothy with Paul's customary greeting of grace and peace. Then thanks is given for the Christian community in Thessalonica – for their work and growth in faith, their labour in mutual love, and their steadfastness in hope (1 Thess 1:2-3; 2 Thess 1:3-4). This theme of love, faith and hope features in other letters of Paul, e.g. Colossians 1:4-5 and Romans 5:1-5. It may have been part of the Church's tradition which Paul inherited on his conversion. For Paul they were not separate realities in Christ – they are integrally inter-linked:

- faith must show itself in loving action and look forward in hope;
- love must be based on faith hoping for what Christ has promised;
- hope is based on faith in what Christ has done and our life in love.

Love and hope are the signs that our faith relationship in and with Christ is alive and well.

Paul was always ready to praise the good aspects in local Christian communities. He even tried to give them a specific designation. He called the Thessalonian community 'our glory and joy' (1 Thess 2:19). They had received the Gospel in much affliction and persecution and with joy inspired by the Holy Spirit so that they became an example to all Christians in Macedonia and the neighbouring province of Achaia. The Gospel had sounded forth from Thessalonica across these provinces and beyond, presumably into the rest of Greece (1 Thess 1:8-9) and Paul could boast of their example to the other Christian churches (2 Thess 1:4).

The main purpose of Paul's correspondence with Thessalonica was to clarify the Parousia (Greek, meaning presence), i.e. the return of Christ, his presence with them again. Both letters deal with this issue, and the phrase 'now concerning' (1 Thess 4:13; 2 Thess 2:1) indicates that the Christians in Thessalonica were seeking information from Paul on this matter (see the phrase in 1 Cor 7:1, 25; 8:1; 12:1; 16:1).

Paul had probably preached an imminent expectation of Christ's return in glory. After he left Thessalonica Christians died and Christ had not returned. This gave rise to concern and doubts. Paul's response was a message of hope and clarification. He focussed on the death and resurrection of Jesus, and then distinguished the Christians who had died from those still alive. At the Parousia 'the dead in Christ will rise first; then we who are alive, who are left, shall be caught up together with them... to meet the

41

Lord... and so we shall always be with the Lord... comfort one another with these words' (1 Thess 4:16-18). Paul at this stage was expecting the Parousia before he died. As for the time of this event he used a phrase reminiscent of Jesus in Matthew 24: 'The day of the Lord [the day of the Parousia] will come like a thief in the night' (1 Thess 5:2).

Someone, or some group, was taking advantage of the confusion over the Parousia to attack Paul and unsettle the Christians in Thessalonica, even trying to break their loyalty to Paul, which happened in Corinth and Galatia. In the second letter Paul asked them 'not to be quickly shaken in mind or excited, either by word or by letter purporting to be from us to the effect that the day of the Lord has come. Let no one deceive you in any way' (2 Thess 2:2-3). It looks as if letter forgery was being used to deceive Christians about the Parousia, and Paul had to take the stylus from the hand of the scribe (probably Silas/Silvanus: see 2 Pet 5:12) and append his signature.

I, Paul, write this greeting with my own hand.
This is the mark in every letter of mine;
it is the way I write (2 Thess 3:17).

What was behind the statement 'that the day of the Lord has come' (2 Thess 2:2)? Here we can detect the difficulty Greek converts had with Christ's resurrection in which Christians share. The Greek mind believed in immortality of the soul, i.e. a pre-existing immortal soul embodied in time and space seeks release and return to heaven. This view emphasised the importance of the spiritual soul, and what happens in the body is not important. Applied to Christianity this could lead to the view that with the gift of Christ's Spirit Christians had achieved the spiritual high-way to heaven and there was no need for a return of Christ as judge of the world because the body/flesh was irrelevant. This view could lead to extremes of asceticism or promiscuity among Christians as it did in Corinth.

Paul's teaching was rooted in the Jewish belief of God's creation in time of the human person created from matter with God's Spirit in the image and likeness of the Creator. This view holds spirit/soul and body together ensuring that what is done in the body has spiritual consequences. But Paul linked resurrection with immortality in that the whole resurrected person's destiny is with God in Christ in heaven. He believed that here and now we share in Christ's presence but the fullness of this presence will come when Christ returns in glory. It was important to get the balance right because Christian thinking and understanding has ramifications in the way Christians live.

It is not accidental that Paul immediately moves from the deceiver/deception in the community at Thessalonica to the Great Deceiver/Deception preceding the Parousia (2 Thess 2:1-12). Paul reminds them of the signs expected before the Parousia: an age of rebellion against God, and the emergence of the 'man of Lawlessness... the son of perdition [assisted by Satan]... takes his seat in the temple of God, proclaiming himself to be God (2 Thess 2:3-4).

God's punishment in the period of final deception would be a 'strong delusion' making people believe what is false so that they do not love and believe the truth – they will be unrighteous (2 Thess 2:11-12). But the Parousia will involve Christ slaying the anti-Christ, i.e. the Son of Perdition. Paul is moving in the same scenario as John in the Book of Revelation, which describes the last great apostasy (lapse of faith) and onslaught of Satan before the final destruction of evil:

And when the thousand years are ended, Satan will be loosed from his prison... to deceive the nations (Rev 20:7-8).

The Man of Lawlessness is akin to the anti-Christ of John (see 1 Jn 2:18; 4:3), whose father is Satan attempting to usurp the rights of God even to the extent of enthroning himself in Jerusalem's temple. This man is probably based on Daniel 7:25, 8:25 and 9:36 where a wicked king is described putting himself above God and profaning the Jewish temple. The Book of Daniel is describing the Greek Seleucid king Antiochus Epiphanes (175-163 BC) who declared himself to be Zeus by setting up an image and altar to Zeus (himself) in Jerusalem's temple, which sparked off the Maccabean revolt of 167 BC.

In 40 AD the Roman emperor, Caligula, had attempted to set up a statue of himself in the temple which provoked riots. So there were precedents for Paul's speculation/ prediction. It seemed only a matter of time before a powerful emperor repeated the desecration of the temple imposing deception and false worship (idolatry). This was the century of Rome's apex of power and emperors arrogating the title of deity to themselves.

It is possible that Paul foresaw another emperor who would warrant the title 'Son of Perdition' coming with Satan's power with pretentious signs and wonders establishing his altar and image in the temple and causing a great apostasy. As a punishment for faithlessness God would send upon those who refused to believe/live the truth a strong delusion making them incapable of distinguishing truth from falsehood. They would believe/live what is false.

Paul did not underestimate the power of evil in society. Evil is a force in man and the world sapping people's moral fibre leading them into a world of deception and lies. The outcome of apostasy/unfaithfulness is a whole atmosphere and cultural ethos working against truth and goodness.

Paul was not pessimistic:

We are bound to give thanks to God always for you... beloved by the Lord, because God chose you... to be saved, through sanctification by the Spirit and belief in the truth... so that you may obtain the glory of... Jesus Christ (2 Thess 2:13-14).

The glory of Jesus Christ – not the glory of emperors!

The second main concern of the correspondence was Christians not working:

> We have heard that some of you are living in idleness, mere busybodies, not doing any work (2 Thess 3:11).

He had made a passing reference to this issue in the first letter; obviously to no effect:

> Admonish the idle (1 Thess 5:14).

This had been a problem even when Paul was with them in Thessalonica, and he had advised 'No work, no food':

> Even when we were with you, we gave you this command: If any one will not work, let him not eat... such persons we command and exhort in the Lord Jesus Christ... to earn their own living...
> If any one refuses to obey what we say... note that man, and have nothing to do with him, that he may be ashamed. Do not look on him as an enemy, but warn him as a brother (2 Thess 3:10-15).

Paul was seeking to correct an abuse in the Christian community stemming from the imminent expectation of the Parousia, correcting the faulty view that since Christ is coming soon it is best to spend all the time in prayer. In practice this would have placed a stressful burden on the Christian community, and played into the hands of opponents branding the Christians as idlers.

Paul appeals to his own example when he was with them in Thessalonica:

> You remember our labour and toil... we worked night and day, that we might not burden any of you (1 Thess 2:9).

Paul was not idle – he worked day and night at his

leather trade and still preached the Gospel. Paul and his missionary companions could have claimed 'board and lodgings' from the community, but they refrained: 'we might have made demands as apostles' (1 Thess 2:6).

Both letters end with 'grace and peace' as they had opened, plus a farewell greeting. The peace he wishes them comes from the God/Lord of peace. The Hebrew word for peace was *shalom*, which really means 'make peace'. This was Paul's background and basis of understanding peace. Peace is a gift from God. It is an active gift – it is a gift of peace-making as lived out par excellence by Jesus. Peace was wished in greeting to the Christian communities, and Paul was praying and hoping that they would be centres of peace-making even amidst persecution and their own internal problems as they waited for the coming of the Lord.

Be at peace among yourselves...
encourage the faint-hearted,
help the weak...
always seek to do good to one another and to all.
Rejoice always,
pray constantly,
give thanks in all circumstances;
for this is the will of God in Christ Jesus for you (1 Thess 5:13-18).

6

Paul's postcard to Philemon

The shortest letter of St Paul in the New Testament is to Philemon, his beloved fellow worker in Christ. It was written about 57 AD from a friend to a friend. More accurately, it is to Philemon, Apphia (his wife?), Archippus (his son?) and 'the church in your house'. The *New Jerusalem Bible* calls it 'a very short note', and it has even been called 'a postcard' (J.J. Greehy). But its brevity belies its importance. It was like a 'spiritual nuclear bomb' in a Roman society based on slavery, and is relevant to our century which has seen slavery on a vast scale in gulags and concentration camps.

Paul wrote from prison: 'I, Paul, a prisoner for Christ.' Three places are usually proposed for the place of imprisonment – Rome, Caesarea in Palestine and Ephesus. We know from Luke in the Acts of the Apostles that Paul was imprisoned in Caesarea, and under house arrest in Rome. There is no mention of imprisonment in Ephesus, yet Ephesus in modern Turkey seems to make best sense as the place from which the letter was sent.[1]

The 'postcard' concerns Philemon's runaway slave, Onesimus, who had ended up with the Apostle from wherever he wrote the card. Colossae, where Philemon probably lived, was only about a hundred miles from Ephesus, a distance a runaway slave might cover without capture. How could a fugitive make it to Rome or Caesarea, journeys which took weeks? And why would a runaway slave want to go to Rome of all places?

Onesimus must have had a very good reason for running away from Philemon's household since his master was noted for kindness. He must have heard Paul preaching and teaching Christ's Gospel of freedom in Philemon's house-church. Paul was on familiar enough terms with Philemon to ask him to 'prepare a guest room for me' because he hoped eventually to visit him. If Onesimus had heard Paul teaching that in Christ there is neither slave nor free person (Gal 3:28), then he might have decided to follow Paul, hoping to gain this freedom and, who knows, even political and economic freedom through Paul's influence with Philemon.

It is estimated that about ninety per cent of the Roman Empire were slaves. The lowest slaves rowed the galley ships and worked mines. They had a short life – a mitigated death sentence. The highest slaves could hold positions of trust and responsibility in the house of free citizens and the wealthy. Owners of slaves could grant them their freedom or allow them to save up money to purchase their freedom, a procedure which focussed on the local temples. It is interesting to note that Onesimus seems to have stolen something from Philemon:

> If he... owes you anything, charge that to my account... I, Paul, write this with my own hand, I will repay it (vv 18-19).

Paul at this point in dictating the letter took the stylus from the scribe and wrote in his own hand 'I will repay'.

Onesimus would have needed money for his flight, but in a 'flight of fancy' did he think that he might be able to purchase his freedom through Paul's good offices? Paul certainly took this act of theft very seriously to write 'I will repay'. Onesimus was doubly guilty in Roman law: he was a runaway slave and a thief.

Powerful appeal

A man named Tychicus seems to have been the bearer of the 'postcard' and in charge of taking Onesimus back to Philemon. In verse 12 Paul says: 'I am sending him (Onesimus) back to you', and if we cross-reference Paul's letter to Colossae, we find Paul sending Onesimus with Tychicus:

Tychicus... I have sent you... and with him Onesimus (Col 4:7-9).

Paul would have had an obligation to send the runaway back since he was Philemon's 'property'. It was a serious offence for a slave to take flight. Special soldiers were assigned to track the slave down and return the fugitive to the owner, who decided on the punishment – crucifixion or branding F (*fugitivum*/fugitive) on the forehead. Branding was the lenient punishment, ensuring the slave would never travel very far again without being sighted.[2]

Paul, who held Roman citizenship, may have persuaded a magistrate to let him take responsibility for getting Onesimus back to Philemon.[3] Paul entrusted this assignment to Tychicus who took the private letter to friend Philemon and a public letter to the church at Colossae. In both letters Mark, Demas, Luke, Aristarchus and Epaphras send greetings. It was as if Paul was saying to Philemon that all these fellow Christians, whom he knew, shared Paul's concern for Onesimus, who was being taken back to await his fate. But what a fate awaited Onesimus!

I, Paul, an ambassador and now a prisoner also for Christ Jesus – I appeal to you for my child, Onesimus, whose [spiritual] father I have become in my imprisonment... I am sending him back to you, *sending my very heart*... that you might have him back for ever, no longer as a slave but more than a slave, as a *beloved brother*... If you consider me your partner, receive him as you would receive me (vv. 9-17).

This must rank as one of the most moving and powerful appeals in history from an old man for his spiritual child (perhaps an indication that Onesimus was quite young). Three times Paul refers to himself being a prisoner. Paul himself was the victim of oppression and appealed from this situation to the free-standing citizen Philemon, whose name included the Greek word *philos* (love). Paul called Philemon 'beloved fellow worker' who was noted for his love (*agape* – the Christian word for Christ's love) and faith towards Christ and all the saints (Christians). Philemon was a good-hearted Christian, and the implication of the letter is that Paul knows he would not misplace his trust in him by sending back the runaway Onesimus. Paul was 'confident of your obedience. I write to you knowing that you will do even more than I say.'

Onesimus 'teamed up' with Paul some time after running away. Did he catch up with Paul on the Roman road from Colossae to Ephesus? Did he take refuge in the temple of the goddess Artemis in Ephesus, and contact Paul from this sanctuary for runaway slaves? Or did they find themselves in the same prison for different reasons? We can only speculate on the circumstances of their meeting, but from the 'postcard' we know that Onesimus had become a Christian on contacting Paul. Paul had become the slave's spiritual father, and thus Onesimus was Philemon's spiritual brother in Christ. Paul's confidence in sending Onesimus back was rooted in the faith and love in Christ which all three of them shared. Paul was bringing the two converts together in Christ – master and slave were now brothers in the Lord.

There is a subtle play on the name 'Onesimus' in the postcard. 'Onesimus' means 'useful' or 'profitable', so Paul writes:

Formerly, he (Onesimus) was useless (non-profitable) but now he is indeed useful to you and to me (as a Christian). Yes, brother, I want some benefit from you in the Lord (vv. 11, 20).

People have wondered why Paul did not denounce slavery in this postcard. He did not suggest that Philemon give Onesimus his political and social freedom. Reasons for Paul's silence could include the utter futility of encouraging revolt. Any individual revolt would have led to crucifixion, and any general rising would have gone the same way as the Spartacus uprising. Christianity would have been branded as subversive treason.

What Paul did in this letter, and in his advice on slaves and masters in Colossians 3:32-4:1, was to stress the new relationship between people in which the external differences of slave and free, Jew and Gentile, male and female, were meaningless in Christ since they are all one (Gal 3:28). When Onesimus went back to Philemon, Paul was saying that the names 'master' and 'slave' became irrelevant. If the master treated the slave as Christ would have treated him, and if the slave served the master as he would serve Christ, then it does not matter if you call one the master and the other the slave: their relationship does not depend on human classification – they are both in Christ. Christianity introduced a new relationship into human affairs in which the human grades of society cease to matter. This good news in the postcard to Philemon still applies today if 'the grace of the Lord Jesus Christ be with your spirit' (v. 23).

Postscript

Ignatius, Bishop of Antioch in Syria, on his way to be martyred in Rome about 110 AD stopped at Smyrna, forty miles from Ephesus. A group of Ephesian Christians, led by their bishop Onesimus, went to greet him. Ignatius gave them a letter to take back to their church. He wrote: 'Onesimus... told me that truth is the guiding principle of your lives.' Was Bishop Onesimus Philemon's ex-slave? we don't know; but it would make a good ending to the story if he had become bishop of Ephesus, and included the postcard from Paul in his collection of Paul's letters for the Christians in Ephesus and district.

NOTES

[1] Luke does not tell us everything about Paul. He relates one flogging and one shipwreck, whereas Paul in 2 Corinthians 11 says he was beaten eight times and shipwrecked on three occasions. Luke does not even relate Paul's imprisonment and martyrdom in Rome. He does record a serious riot in Ephesus due to Paul's conversion work (Acts 19). Paul himself relates serious trouble in Asia and its religious capital, Ephesus. He fought with beasts at Ephesus (1 Cor 15:32), and God delivered him from deadly peril in Asia (2 Cor 1:8-19).

[2] The ancient Roman writer Tacitus records a Roman prefect being assassinated by one of his slaves. Roman law required the execution of the offending slave and the whole slave-household with him. Four hundred slaves were crucified.

[3] It is possible that Philemon had not initiated 'chase' of Onesimus, and Paul had heard of his good-hearted gesture. In this case, Paul would not have needed a magistrate's permission to send him back. Philemon and Paul were 'covering up' the theft and flight in the Spirit of Christ.

7

Paul: faithful faith

In the time of Paul Colossae (perhaps named after Lake Koloe) was a small city in the Lycus Valley in the Roman province of Asia (modern Turkey). The city was controlled by a proconsul, responsible to the Senate in Rome, whose headquarters were in Ephesus, 125 miles to the west. Colossae was on the main Roman road from Ephesus to the east and formed a triangular network with the neighbouring cities of Hierapolis and Laodicea. It is an area of potential earthquakes. In the early 60s AD the three cities were hit by quakes. But Paul's letter to the Christians in Colossae and neighbouring Laodicea written about 57 AD was concerned with a potential devastation of their faith.[1]

From what Paul writes in his letter to Colossae he does not appear to have visited the city or Laodicea:

I want you to know how greatly I strive for you, and for those at Laodicea, and for all who have not seen my face (Col 2:1).

In Acts Luke does not record Paul evangelising in these cities. But Luke does say that through Paul's preaching in the Hall of Tyranus in Ephesus over two years 'all the residents of Asia heard the word of the Lord, both Jews and Greeks' (Acts 19:10). The silversmith Demetrius, at the time of the anti-Christian riot in Ephesus, says: 'throughout all Asia this Paul has persuaded and turned away a considerable company of people' (Acts 19:26) from worshipping the mother goddess Artemis.

The link-man between Paul and the three Lycus Valley cities was Epaphras of Colossae 'who worked hard for you [Colossae] and for those in Laodicea and Hierapolis' (Col 4:12-13). The implication is that Epaphras had evangelised these cities, and that he himself may have been converted through Paul's preaching in Ephesus:

The gospel which has come to you...
as you learned it from Epaphras...
He... has made known to us your love in the Spirit...
for all the saints... we have heard of your faith in Christ... (Col 1:5-8.4)

Epaphras had reported to Paul on the state of the Church in Colossae and district emphasising their faith and love, which enabled Paul to call Epaphras 'our be*love*d servant... *faithful* minister of Christ' (Col 1:7).

Paul wrote to Colossae from prison (Col 4:10.18). Epaphras and Aristarchus of Thessalonica were fellow prisoners (Col 4:10; Philem v. 23). The letter was sent out in the names of Paul and Timothy (Col 1:1) and contains greetings from Aristarchus, Epaphras, Luke, Demas (who later abandoned the faith), and Mark (cousin of Barnabas) who had accompanied Paul on his first missionary journey. These five 'greeters' also send good wishes in Paul's letter to Philemon, who lived in or around Colossae. Both letters have an address to Archippus (probably Philemon's son), and both mention Onesimus, Philemon's runaway slave. So the two letters were probably written and sent at the same time from Ephesus.

The postman seems to have been Tychicus whom Paul calls beloved brother, fellow servant and faithful minister, who was taking faithful and beloved Onesimus back to his master Philemon (Col 4:7-8). A third letter appears to have been delivered by Tychicus to Laodicea since in 4:16 Paul says to the Colossians: 'When this letter has been read among you, have it read also in the church of the Laodiceans; and see that you read also the letter from Laodicea.' [2]

Here we see letters circulating in the early Church as a means of communication, and of building up the young churches in faith and love. There is no existing copy of the letter to Laodicea, but it indicates 'lost letters' as Luke's gospel indicates 'lost gospels' (Lk 1:1). Paul probably wrote many letters: some we have as they were written, e.g. Philemon; some have been amalgamated into one long letter, e.g. 2 Corinthians; and some lost, e.g. Laodicea.

Colossians has been described as a letter on how to handle a crisis – a crisis of faith. It has also been seen as a lesson to us today as to how we should respond to the crisis which the Church is passing through in our times.

Paul's opening greeting sounds the note of being faithful. He wishes them grace and peace – his customary greeting in all his letters – and, as in his letters to Rome, Corinth and Philippi, he calls them 'saints' (Greek *hagioi*, meaning 'holy ones'), and adds 'faithful brethren' (1:1). The note of faithful saints also opens the letter to Ephesus, which has links with the letter to Colossae. Just as Romans seems to be an expansion of Galatians, so Ephesians appears to be an expanded development of Colossians.

It is no accident that Paul stresses the faithfulness of Christians associated with Colossae: Epaphras (evangeliser) is a faithful minister (4:7); Tychicus (delegate) also a faithful minister (4:7); even the young runaway slave Onesimus is a faithful brother (4:9). Paul intends them to be examples of faithfulness in faith in Christ.

But Epaphras and Tychicus are no substitutes for Paul himself – they are apostolic delegates (delegates of Paul). He is with the Christians of Colossae in spirit even if absent in body. He is concerned for them that firm in faith they are knit together in community of love and filled with thanksgiving. This will only continue if they are true to the tradition of faith in Christ (Col 2:1-6).

Paul was concerned that the Christians in Colossae were being deluded in faith by beguiling speakers. Since he asked for a mutual exchange of letters between Colossae and Laodicea he must have felt that the delusion in faith could spread. He warned them against being a prey to human wisdom (philosophy) and empty deceit (2:8). So what could have been happening for Paul to caution against delusion, prey, deceit?

Across Colossians 2:6-3:4 Paul gets down to the real business of the letter, i.e. counteracting deceitful knowledge concerning Christ with the consequences for Christian faith and living which could follow. Up to this point in the letter he had hinted concern abut their knowledge in faith in Christ:

> We have not ceased to pray for you, asking that you may be filled with knowledge... spiritual wisdom and understanding... increasing in the knowledge of God....to have... understanding and the knowledge of... Christ in whom are hid the treasures of wisdom and knowledge (1:9-11; 2:2-3).

Knowledge (Greek: *gnosis*) was an 'in word' in Asia at that time. The mystery religions/cults with their secret knowledge and rites were popular. They gave a sense of fellowship and salvation. The secret knowledge was gained through enactment of myth and the sharing of a sacred meal. The secret knowledge concerned the many intermediaries between heaven and earth whom it was necessary to know and understand to gain the way of salvation. There was a whole world of angels in various categories which Paul reflects in 1:15-16, viz. thrones, dominations, principalities and powers in hierarchical order. This is an example of Paul's use of mystery cult thought. Other examples are words such as 'mystery' (2:2), 'fullness' (1:19; 2:9-10), 'hidden' (2:26, 3:3). He had to use the language of the cults to counter their influence because Christ was being reduced to 'top angel', i.e. was being reduced to a divine angelic messenger.

The influence of secret gnostic thought from the

mystery religions on the Christians may have come via pagan converts linked with these cults, and Jewish converts. The centre of the cult of Sabazios was in Phrygia, the area around Colossae. Sabazios was given the attributes of Zeus (Greek supreme god). Some Jews of Phrygia combined the worship of Sabazios with their own god (an unusual practice for Jews). The people around Colossae seem to have believed that all religions had something to offer and should be combined. So the Christians of the area were probably being subjected to the propaganda that it was possible, and desirable, to combine belief in Jesus Christ with the belief and practices of other cults. There were those 'insisting on... worship of angels' (2:18). Applied to Christianity this short-changed Jesus as 'top angel' – it removed him from the sphere of man, and reduced his identification with God.

Paul set out the status of Christ in the powerful hymn in chapter 1 verses 15-20: a hymn he probably incorporated from use in liturgical settings. Whoever composed it drew on the wisdom literature of the Old Testament to produce a Christian wisdom hymn in diptych form (two panels):

Panel 1:
Creation

Christ is the image of God.
First-born of all creation, in whom all things were created in heaven and on earth. Christ is before all things, holding all things together.

Panel 2:
New creation

Christ is the head of the Church.
First-born from the dead.
In him dwells the fullness of God.
All things in heaven and on earth are reconciled through Christ enabling peace through the cross.

Here is the true mystery knowledge and wisdom 'hidden for ages... but now made manifest [revealed] to his saints' (Christians) so that they can 'mature in Christ' (cf 1:25-28).

Faith is only one side of the Christian coin – love (*agape*) is its complementary side. Hence, Paul spells out in some detail what should be happening in the faithful Christian community of Colossae – what should be developing among those who share the life of Christ through baptism (2:12-14). They should be knit together in love, knit and growing through the joints and ligaments of the body of Christ (the Church) with Christ as Head (2:2, 19).

Faulty faith brings faulty living as a Christian. This was happening in Colossae. Faulty emphasis on Jesus as 'top angel' was leading some Christians to live according to the standards of the world (2:20). In spite of apparent devotion and ascetical practices there was indulgence of the flesh (2:23). So Paul went into a series of contrasts between life in the flesh and life in the Spirit. Unfortunately, texts of the Bible do not allow the fascinating style of Paul's mind and writing to stand out clearly. Here is how Paul in general contrasts the life-styles of those in Christ and those glued to earthly/worldly wavelengths:

Seek things above
Set mind on things above

Put to death	fornication	
	impurity	
	passion	
	evil desire	
	covetousness	– idolatrous life
Put away	anger	
	wrath	
	malice	
	slander	
	foul talk	– lying life
	the old nature	

58

Put on	*the new nature*
	the image of the Creator being
	renewed in knowledge [3]
Put on	compassion
	kindness
	lowliness
	meekness
	patience – a life of forbearance
Above all	
Put on	love – which binds in
	harmony
Let	the peace of Christ rule in your hearts
Let	the word of Christ dwell in you

                                        (3:1-16)

'Putting to death' and 'putting on' have baptismal connotations – the convert casting aside the old nature (life-style) symbolised by the old daily clothes, walking down into the baptismal water (symbolising the tomb and death of Christ); then rising out of the water in the resurrection of Christ putting on a white robe symbolising the new nature, the new life-style in Christ. Paul had already reminded them of the meaning and significance of baptism in 2:12-13:

> You were buried with him [Christ] in baptism, in which you were also raised with him...
> You... were dead in trespasses [sin]... made alive together with him, having forgiven us all our trespasses.

Baptism was probably followed by the Lord's Supper (the Eucharist) making up the 'Christian mysteries'.

A striking feature of Colossians is that throughout it Paul emphasises the uniqueness and all-sufficiency of Christ. Christ's supreme position in relation to all forces and powers claiming to influence human life and destiny is stressed. Christ has no rivals such as planetary powers (astrology) or angels (2:16-18).

It has been said that this letter contains the highest reach of Paul's Christian thought written to so unimportant a city as Colossae. But in so doing he checked a tendency, a faulty teaching in faith, which if allowed to continue would have wrecked Asian Christianity, and which might have damaged the faith of the wider Church.

The last faithful word can be left to Paul:

As... you received Christ... so live in him, rooted and built up in him and established in the faith, just as you were taught (2:6-7).

NOTES

[1] All dating in the New Testament is approximate. The dating of Colossians depends on whether it was written from Rome or Ephesus. Colossians links with Philemon and makes sense from Ephesus about 57 AD.

[2] A fourth letter could have been taken by Tychicus. Analysis of Ephesians suggests it was a circular letter rather than specifically for Ephesus. Chapter 6 verse 21 says Tychicus was being sent, i.e. sent out from Ephesus presumably with the letter we call Ephesians.

[3] Old/new natures. The literal translation of the Greek is old/new man.

Old man = Adam of the earth   distorting man's image / trespasser / guilty of idolatry / life in the flesh.

New man = Christ of heaven   image of God / reconciler / enabling renewal of man's true image / life in the Spirit.

8

Paul's vision of the Church

To the saints who are at Ephesus and faithful to Christ Jesus
(cf Eph 1:1)

This greeting is found only in some ancient manuscripts:
it is not in the most reliable ones. This suggests that the
original letter may have had a blank space for the name of
the church in which it was being read to be inserted. If this
was true then the so-called letter to Ephesus would have
been a circular letter. It is a letter written from prison (Eph
3:1, 4:1), perhaps at the same time as the letter to Colossae,
and delivered to various churches en route by Tychicus,
who was 'postman' to Colossae (Col 4:7). Tychicus is the
only person mentioned in Ephesians (6:21). The link between the two letters is considerable. Some three-fifths of
Ephesians is similar material to that in Colossians, giving
rise to the view that the letter circulating as Ephesians was
an expanded version of Colossians.

If Ephesians was a circular letter to the young Asian
churches then it could be regarded as a manifesto giving
them hope and encouragement to be Church. It shows the
benefits that the Christian faith, and being in Christ, has to
offer to all mankind, the place of the Church in God's
purposes, and what is involved in living as a Christian. The
key wavelength is the gathering of all things in Christ, who
is the centre of all things, and the head who unites all
things.

Ephesians marks a high point in the devotional literature of the Church and has been called a poem in prose.

Some regard it as the high point of New Testament thought, and it has been called 'Queen of the Letters'. It falls into two main sections:

1. Christ is God's instrument of reconciliation (chapters 1-3);

2. The Church is Christ's instrument of reconciliation (chapters 4-6).

The letter style of Ephesians begins in 1:1 and continues with 1:15. The verses in between (1:3-14) are like a hymn stating the themes to be covered in the letter, viz.:

Praise of God	v. 3
God's loving gracious plan	vv. 4-6
God's forgiveness through Christ	vv. 6-7
God's revelation concerning the unity of all things	vv. 9-10
which is shared by all Christians	vv. 11-14

Paul moves on in a trinitarian wavelength (v. 17) to the vision of the Church as the body of Christ embracing the universe:

God raised Christ from the dead, and made him sit at his right hand... and he has put all things under his feet and has made him the head over all things for the church, which is his body, the fullness of him who fills all in all (1:20-22).[1]

Chapter 2:1-10 has been called a 'lyric of love' in which Paul pours out his heart at the wonder of God's grace (Christ) in relation to sinful mankind. 'You' in the passage refers to Gentiles, 'us' to Jews. Before Christ's coming the Gentiles were spiritually dead, likewise the Jews in their life in the circumcised flesh. The word Paul uses for sin is *hamartia*, a shooting term, meaning 'a miss'. Sin is missing the mark of who we ought to be. Both Jew and Gentile had not become who they should have been – not realised

62

their potential to be sons and daughters in the image and likeness of God. But 'God... is rich in mercy', loving with a great love, and saving the human race by the free gift of Christ (grace): 'By grace you have been saved through faith' (v. 8). Christians have become God's work and should walk in Christ's good works.[2]

Paul continues highlighting the miracle which has come about in Christ with Jew and Gentile coming together in Christ in community. The Jews had an immense contempt for the Gentiles – they were unclean and to be shunned. If a Jew married a Gentile a funeral was carried out to signify that the Jew was dead to God and the Chosen People. To Jews the Gentiles were hopeless people; aliens with no part in God's purposes, limited to the world, without God, without hope. If they visited the temple in Jerusalem they were confined to the outer court of the Gentiles. Any move beyond the screen-barrier incurred the death penalty. With Christ's coming removed this dividing marble screen:

Christ ... is our peace, who has made us both one, and has broken down the dividing wall of hostility (2:14).

The divisive Jew-Gentile religious barrier with its social and political consequences was removed so that God in Christ 'might create... one new man in place of the two (Gentile man and Jewish man)... and might reconcile us both to God in one body through the cross, thereby bringing the hostility to an end (2:15-16, 4:22-24). Paul uses the Greek word *kainos* for 'new', which means a new quality – a new quality of man and woman is possible in community in Christ.

The new man, the new Adam is Christ (Rom 5:12-21; 1 Cor 15:21). Jew and Gentile, by coming into Christ in Christian community, become a people with a new quality (Spirit) of life. They become united, they are 'at one', they make peace (Hebrew word *shalom*).

Paul uses the image of a building (a temple) to explain the Church. Christ is the cornerstone. Every Christian is like a stone built into the building (temple – Church). The building is an on-going process being constructed as 'dwelling place of God in the Spirit' (2:22). To the Christians in Corinth Paul wrote: 'We are temples of the living God' (2 Cor 6:16); your body is a temple of the Holy Spirit within you, which you have from God' (1 Cor 6:19).

In 4:1-16 Paul calls for unity in the churches to which he writes. Behind these verses lie three different threats to unity:

1. Arguments between Christians. The antidote is love in the Spirit based on the sevenfold structure of unity, i.e. one Body, one Spirit, one hope, one Lord, one faith, one baptism, one God.

2. Diversity of services within the Church. As the Church spread there was a mushrooming of ministries and this involved questions of authority, which was a pastoral issue of how the various gifts and ministries were to function for the well-being of the Christian communities.

In 1 Corinthians 12, Paul lists nine gifts of the Spirit (vv. 4-11) which are co-related with eight services of Christ in the Christian communities (vv. 27-30). The gifts of wisdom, knowledge and faith are linked to apostles, prophets and teachers in this rank order which is stressed by 'first, second and third'. Then comes miracle-workers, healers, helpers, administrators and speakers/interpreters of tongues. In Ephesians the gifts of the Spirit in the community are co-related to five services:

Christ's gifts... were that some should be apostles, some prophets, some evangelists, some pastors, and teachers to equip the saints, for the work of ministry, for building up the body of Christ [i.e. the Church] (Eph 4:7-12).

The gifts in the Christian communities are for the building up of everybody in fellowship in Christ. In 1 Corinthians 12:4-7 in a trinitarian passage Paul makes clear whose gifts they are:

There are varieties of gifts, but the same Spirit ; and there are varieties of service, but the same Lord (Christ) ... there are varieties of working, but it is the same God who inspires them all in every one. To each is *given* the manifestation of the Spirit for the common good.

Further on comes the famous parallelling of the importance of the unity of the parts of the human body and the unity of the members who make up the Church and local churches (1 Cor 12:12-31). It has been described as one of the most famous pictures of the unity of the Church that has ever been written. Paul makes the points that those in Christian community need each other, and that each person has a part to play in the Church. Weaker members (weak in faith – perhaps the sick) are indispensable, and the 'less honourable' Christians (perhaps slaves, the poor, etc.) are to be honoured. There is to be no discord but care for everyone. If one suffers, all suffer; if one is honoured, all rejoice.

3. Unorthodox teaching. The remedy is to speak the truth in love, and grow up in every way into Christ who is the head of the Church. Only in this way will the Church grow and be built up in love.

Across 5:21-33 Paul uses his third metaphor/picture for the Church. He has spoken of the Church as Christ's body of which he is the head: of the Church as a building (temple) with Christ as the cornerstone: now Christ is the bridegroom with the Church as his bride. This section is a beautiful interflow parallelling Christ's relationship with his Church and the relationship of husband and wife. In a world which demeaned woman and was rampant with divorce these verses reflect the beacon of light of those married in Christ.

Ephesians 5:21-33 has been given a 'bad press' suggesting Paul believed in man's dominance over his wife. Nothing is more untrue. The basis of the passage is love, not control. It opens on the key note of mutual service to each other: 'Be subject to one another out of reverence for

Christ.' Three times Paul exhorts husbands to love their wives as Christ loved the Church, as they love themselves and their own bodies. Three times he exhorts wives:

be subject to husband as to Christ,
be subject to husband as the Church is to Christ,
respect your husband (something they found difficult in a permissive society).

Paul was treading a diplomatic road in Christ in his advice to the married in Christ. On the one hand he had to avoid facing accusations of undermining the structures of marriage if he emphasised neither male nor female in Christ (Gal 3:28). On the other hand Christ had brought a revolution in human relationships. Just as the terrible barrier between Jew and Gentile goes in Christ so does society's barriers between man and woman which disadvantages woman. So husband and wife are to love and serve one another in the Spirit of Christ's loving service of his Church.

Christ as head of the Church is another clue as to the revolutionary wavelength Paul was working on in Christ. 'Head' in biblical thought concerns source and origin. So:

God	is head of	Christ
Christ	is head of	Church
Man/husband	is head of	woman/wife

This is not a chain of domination but of love, gift and mutual service. How we interpret this important passage will depend on how we understand Paul's thought in general, and how he was seeking through preaching and teaching the Word (Christ) of God to allow the Spirit to change relationships and remove barriers of dominance and division which mar people's lives.

Two more 'barrier issues' follow the passage on marriage: children and parents, masters and slaves. Children (teenage and adult) are to obey and respect their ageing parents (fourth commandment). Neglect of parents seems to be a feature of permissive societies. On the other hand fathers are not to provoke their children to anger with all the consequences for family life which can result from 'the heat of the moment' (6:1-4).

An estimated ninety percent of people in the Roman empire in the first century AD were slaves. Christianity's message of freedom would have appealed to such a situation bringing many slaves into the Christian communities. Paul's letter to Philemon changed the nature of master-slave relationship but the outward structures continued. In dealing with this delicate situation Paul had to have the wisdom of Solomon to avoid charges of sedition (the previous century had seen the revolt of slaves under Spartacus). In Ephesians 6:5-9 and Colossians 3:22-4:1, Paul gives the same advice to masters and slaves. Slaves are to obey their masters as slaves of Christ (Paul called himself a slave of Christ; cf Rom 1:1), giving service as to Christ. Masters are to render service and fairness to slaves as to Christ. They are to remember that they have a Master in heaven who has no favourites.

Paul was under no illusion as to the kind of world he lived in: 'the days are evil' (Eph 5:11), and he advised the Christians to 'look carefully... how you walk',[2] '... take no part part in the unfruitful works of darkness, but... expose them' (5:11), '... you must no longer live as the Gentiles do... alienated from the life of God... they have become callous, and have given themselves up to licentiousness' (4:17-19).

Paul appreciated that the Christian and Christian community are involved in a spiritual war against the forces of darkness. His letter reaches its climax in a plea to the Christians to put on the armour of Christ. He probably looked at the Roman soldier guarding him as he described the spiritual armour of God:

cuirass (loin cover)	of truth
breastplate	of righteousness
sandals	of peace
shield	of faith
helmet	of salvation
sword	of the Spirit

Like a Roman officer he gave three commands:

Be strong in Christ;
Stand, i.e. give no ground;
Pray at all times in the Spirit.

But the spiritual war from the Christian side is rooted into Christ's reconciling role in the world through the Church and its local communities:

Be kind to one another, tenderhearted,
forgiving one another, as God in Christ forgave you
(4:32).

NOTES

[1] Imagery of the ancient world where a king or emperor sometimes co-ruled with his designated son-successor. Christ, God's Son, co-rules the kingdom of God with the Father.

[2] Theme of 'The Way' – the designation for the Christian life-style of the Christian communities (Acts 9:2, 22:4, 24:14, 22). Also, Way of salvation (Acts 16:17), Way of the Lord (Acts 18:25), 'I am the Way' (Jn 14:6).

9

Christ and the Christian

The Letter to the Romans

It is not known who first took Christianity to Rome. The earliest indication outside the New Testament is found in Suetonius' book *The Twelve Caesars*:

Because the Jews at home caused continuous disturbances at the instigation of Chrestus, Claudius expelled them from the city.

Claudius reigned from 41-54 AD and this expulsion is thought to have been about 48 AD due to heated debate between Jews and the claims of Jewish Christians for Christ. Since only foreign Jews could be expelled without trial the presumption is that it was Jews and Jewish Christians from this group who were ordered out of Rome.

When Paul, Aristarchus and possibly Luke arrived at Puteoli, port of Rome, they stayed there with the Christian community. As they journeyed along the Appian Way to Rome itself, a deputation of Roman Christians met them at the Forum of Appius (43 miles) and at the Three Taverns (33 miles from Rome). Paul's reputation and his long letter to them written from Corinth over two years previously had made their mark. No wonder, because the letter to Rome is regarded as his masterpiece enlightening and revolutionising Christians down the centuries.

Paul had written about 58 AD from Gaius' house in Corinth telling the Christians in Rome that he hoped to see them on his way to Spain, 'and to be sped (helped) on my journey there by you, once I have enjoyed your company for a little' (Rom 15:24). But there were other reasons for Paul wanting to visit the imperial city. It was the capital of a vast empire with all the main highways leading to and from Rome. So Paul was eager to preach the gospel 'For I long to see you, that I may be mutually encouraged by each other's faith... in order that I may reap some harvest among you as well as among the rest of the Gentiles' (Rom 1:11-13. It would have taken weeks to write since scribing with stylus on parchment was a slow task. The 'postwoman' was probably Phoebe, a deaconess of the church of Cenchreae, Aegean port of Corinth. When she arrived in Rome she probably stayed at the house of Aquila and Priscilla (Rom 16:3). They would have known each other from the days when Prisca and Aquila lived and worked with Paul in Corinth (Acts 18:1-2), but Paul asked the whole community to 'receive her in the Lord as befits the saints, and help her in whatever she may require from you, for she has been a helper of many and myself' (Rom 16:2).

The sixteen chapters of Romans can be put into four divisions:

(i)   1-8   The problem of being in a right relationship with God (righteousness).

(ii)   9-11   The problem of the Jews (the Chosen People) rejecting Christ.

(iii) 12-15 Issues of Christian living.

(iv) 16   A letter or appendix of introduction for Phoebe.

Chapters 9-11 break the flow of the letter. They form a compact unit on their own, and it has been suggested that originally they were a treatise used by Paul for dealing with the issue of why the Chosen People, as a people, had rejected Jesus as God's Messiah (Christ). These chapters can be read without reference to the rest of the letter and this may be a useful way to read them. They emphasise the mercy of God.

Ancient manuscripts of Romans reveal a variety of 'end points'. The present ending 16:25-27 is a doxology and in most good manuscripts this is where it is found. But some have the doxology at the end of chapter 14, and one manuscript at the end of chapter 15. The clue to these variations may lie in a manuscript which leaves out 'in Rome' in the first chapter (1:7, 15) suggesting that the letter became a circular like Ephesians. In this context chapters 15 and 16 could be left out according to where the letter was circulating, and the doxology could be duly placed at the appropriate end point.

In the light of all these possibilities a survey on the basis of chapters 1-8 followed by 12-14 ending with the doxology of 16:25-27 can be undertaken.

Commentaries tackle Romans 1-8 in two main ways: chapter by chapter or a series of divisions and subdivisions. Both approaches are not very helpful for readers seeking to get to grips with the heart of the matter of these chapters in which Paul is getting to the heart of the matter regarding Christ and the Christian. It makes best sense to focus on the three key figures Paul holds up for consideration, i.e. Adam, Abraham and Christ. From Adam comes every man and woman caught up in idolatry (fallen man and woman). From Abraham come the Chosen People and the God-given Law which they are unable to live up to. From Christ comes life in the Spirit which empowers every man and woman to be in a right relationship with God.

Adam and the Gentiles

In 5:12-21, approximately half-way through chapters 1-8, Paul contrasts Adam and Christ. Through Adam (every man) sin and death (pre-eminently spiritual death) came/comes into the world and spreads to all. The disobedient trespass (reference to Eden) of Adam brought condemnation for all men and women. Every man and woman in Adam is out of true relationship with God.

In 1:18-31 Paul points out the consequences for living which flow from this out-of-relationship with the Creator. Man's thinking becomes futile and his mind darkened so that he no longer acknowledges the invisible God in creation. Claiming to be wise, man becomes foolish setting up images of mortal birds, animals and reptiles to worship instead of the immortal God. The truth about God is exchanged for a lie, and creatures are served rather than the Creator!

Instead of a life-style based on love mankind's folly leads to a life-style of lust. Out-of-relationship with God man's and woman's relationships become homosexual and lesbian. The irony is that worship of nature and creature brings unnatural relationships between people.

Paul lists twenty-one anti-social aspects of pagan society (vv. 29-31). The opening line translates literally as 'filled with all unrighteousness' and works its way through evil, murder, God-haters, inventors of evil, disobedience to parents, etc., ending 'without mercy' (ruthless). Paul deliberately opened with 'unrighteousness' and ended 'without mercy' because lack of mercy comes from lack of love which is rooted in a right relationship with God, who is Love.

It might seem as if Paul is getting hysterical in this section. In fact he was very restrained. First-century AD Roman society was a period of unbridled luxury and immorality. It was an age so weary of ordinary things that it was avid for new sensations. Crime became an antidote to boredom. Roman writers themselves decried the state of society: 'the greater the infamy, the wilder the delight' (Tacitus); 'women were married to be divorced, and divorced to be married' (Seneca); chastity was a rare good fortune and 'no guilt or deed of lust is wanting since Roman purity disappeared' (Juvenal). The life-style of the Roman world vividly illustrated life in Adam, what Paul called 'life in the flesh'. The 'glory of Rome' was not the way to the glory of God!

Paul turned to the Chosen People and their reliance on the Law given to Moses, which gave rise to boasting of their relationship with God (2:17). Because they were instructed in God's Law (*Torah*) they were sure they were a guide to the blind and a light to those in darkness, i.e. the pagan Gentiles whom they regarded as foolish children (2:19-20). Paul denounced this false boasting: 'you who boast in the Law... dishonour God by breaking the law' (2:23). They broke the commandments as much as the Gentiles. They were guilty of idolatry (first commandment), adultery (sixth) and stealing (seventh). Paul may have selected these three commandments because they concern God, self and others. They highlight the breakdown of love – love of God, love of self, love of others (cf Mt 22:37-40).

For Paul even the central rite/sign of circumcision was no guarantee that Jews were in a right relationship with God. If they break the Law they are still like the Gentiles even though circumcised. He hammered home the point by stating that the real Jew is one inwardly. Real circumcision (sign of being God's chosen) is spiritual and a matter of the heart. If Gentiles keep God's laws their heart and spirit are right (2:25-29).

Jew and Gentile are under the power of sin (3:9) with all the consequences which follow – spiritual death and life in the flesh (or circumcised flesh). Because of sin the Jews do not have the power within them to keep the Law. Law of itself does not give the power to obey the Law. In chapter 7 Paul speaks from intense personal experience of the inability to keep the Law:

> We know that the law is spiritual; but I am carnal, sold and under sin. I do not understand my own actions. For I do not do what I want, but I do the very thing I hate... It is no longer I that do it, but sin which dwells within me... in my flesh... I can will what is right, but I cannot do it (7:14-18).

This spiritual dilemma applies to the whole human race – it is the fallen human condition. Even God's Law, holy, just and good (7:12) does not solve the problem. In fact it heightens it. The Law increases trespass (5:20) and accountability (5:13), and the power of sin uses the Law to deceive and kill people's spiritual lives (7:11). The deception consists in deluding people that they can achieve their own salvation, whereas the reality is that salvation (getting into a right relationship with God) is a gift from God.

To Jews and Jewish Christians (the Judaisers) preoccupied with Law and righteousness Paul advised getting behind the Law given to Moses, to Abraham, founding father of the Chosen People. He was in a right relationship (righteous) without the Law:

Abraham believed [man of faith],
and it was reckoned to him as righteousness (4:3).

He was in a right relationship with God even before circumcision (4:9-10). He was 'father of all believers', who have faith without circumcision (4:11); and God's promises were made to him when he was righteous in faith long before the Law (4:13). Faith precedes Law in God's plan so that people can see and understand that God's saving activity rests on grace (4:16), i.e. rests in God's free gift in love in the person of Jesus his Son.

Christ and the Christian

Now the righteousness of God has been manifested apart from the law... through faith in Jesus Christ for all who believe. For there is no distinction [between Gentiles and Jews]; since all have sinned and fall short of the glory of God, they are justified [put right] by God's grace as gift, through the redemption [purchase out of slavery to sin] which is in Christ Jesus (3:21-24).

74

So there can be no more self-boasting based on deed/works done according to the Law – no more self-satisfaction in what I have done. The only boasting is in Christ based on faith in what God has done for us (3:27).

Those in Christ, justified by grace through faith, have access to God: have access to the loving encounter with God and all the consequences which follow – peace, joy, God's love poured into our hearts through the Holy Spirit, and hope in sharing God's glory (5:1-5).

In chapter 6 Paul states how baptism initiates us into Christ. Going down into the baptismal waters (symbolising the tomb) we are buried with Christ. Coming out we rise with him and begin to walk in newness of life. In baptism the old sinful life-style (life in the flesh) seen so clearly in the permissive Roman society is crucified[1] and the new life-style (life in the Spirit) lived out by Jesus put on:

> Consider yourselves dead to sin, and alive to God in Christ Jesus (6:11).

Chapter 8 is one of the highpoints of all Paul's writings. It is a profound statement of life in the Spirit, a penetrating insight into the Power (Spirit) of Christ in the Christian. Paul deeply appreciated that we cannot be in a right relationship with God by our own efforts. We need God's Spirit to empower us to live like Jesus. For those with faith in Christ this happens:

> The Spirit of life in Christ Jesus has set me free from the law of sin and death. For God has done what the law, weakened by the flesh, could not do (8:2-3).

Across 8:1-30 Paul maps out the contrasting life-styles of life in the flesh (spirit of slavery to sin) and life in the Spirit (spirit of sonship with God):

75

	Life in the flesh	*Life in the Spirit*
sets mind on which are:	things of the flesh fornication, impurity, licentiousness, idolatry, sorcery, enmity, strife, jealousy, anger, selfishness, dissension, party spirit, envy, drunkenness, carousing	things of the Spirit love, joy, peace patience, goodness kindness, faithfulness, gentleness, self-control (Gal 5:19-22).
life-style of	death hostility to God spiritual death slavery to sin life of fear	life and peace submission to God spiritual life free sons/daughters of God life of hope the Spirit prays within us intercedes for us enables us to call God 'Abba' conforms us to the image of Jesus.

Christian living

In chapters 12-14 Paul applies life in the Spirit to the daily life of Christians in Roman society. He emphasises love and its outflow:

Let love be genuine...
love one another with brotherly [sisterly] affection...
Contribute to the need of the saints,
practise hospitality [important for house-churches]...
Live in harmony with one another...
associate with the lowly...
if your enemy is hungry, feed him;
if he is thirsty, give him drink (12:9-20).

Chapter 13 is advice on how to relate to Roman authority and government. This should be seen in the context of Claudius' expulsion of Jews and Jewish Christians from

Rome in 48 AD and the emergence of Nero as emperor (54-68 AD). Paul was writing about 58 AD when Jewish Christians, like Aquila and Priscilla, had returned to Rome. Paul was concerned that there should be no grounds for Christians being involved in civil strife. Again love is stressed:

love one another; for he who loves his neighbour has fulfilled the law...
love does no wrong to a neighbour...
love is the fulfilling of the law (13:8.10).

He roots all authority in God:

Let every person be subject to the governing authorities. For there is no authority except from God, and those that exist have been instituted by God.... he who resists the authorities resists what God has appointed.... Pay all of them their dues, taxes... revenue... respect to whom respect is due (13:1-7).

Chapter 14 deals with harmony within the Christian communities in Rome. The coming together in community in Christ of Jews and Gentiles brought its problems. The Jewish Christians had a background of strict observance of the Sabbath, and strict regulations regarding certain foods as clean and unclean. There were Jewish converts who wished to continue observing the Sabbath (14:6) and avoid unclean foods (14:13-23). Other converts were vegetarians (14:2), which was a 'fashionable fad' among some Gentile groups. There were those like Paul who followed Jesus in seeing nothing as unclean in itself (14:14). Amid all these variations of views Paul had to find regulating principles in the interests of peace and building up of the communities (14:19). His pastoral advice was:

Not to despise each other
Not to pass judgement on one another
Place no stumbling block [scandal] in anyone's way

Act from faith...
pursue what makes for peace
and for mutual upbuilding...,
do not destroy the work of God [the Christian communities] (vv. 3-20)

In other words do not destroy the astonishing phenomenon of Jews and Gentiles coming together in the Spirit of Christ to be God's loving sign to the world in darkness.

NOTES

[1] The cross was a symbol of the brutality of the idolatrous Roman empire, which had crucified Jesus. Through Christ crucified, and Christians crucifying life in the flesh (the life-style of the empire), genuine love and true worship of God were released through life in the Spirit. Paul was clear about the paradox of the cross: Christ crucified was a stumbling block to Jews and folly to Gentiles; to Christians the power of God, the wisdom of God (1 Cor 1:23-24).

10

Paul's pence for the poor

All dating in the New Testament is notoriously difficult, and Paul's life and times are no exception. The most firm date (fixed point) for New Testament dating relates to Paul's appearance before pro-consul Gallio in Corinth (Acts 18:12-17). From Roman history we know that Gallio was in Corinth for at least a year in 51 AD. In 1905 a stone inscription recording a statement of the emperor Claudius was found in Achaia (Greece) which said:

Claudius, father of the country for the 26th time
Gallio, my friend and consul.

A useful clue for Paul's life is Luke calling him a 'young man' (Greek: *neanias*) at the stoning of Stephen (Acts 7:58). The Greek doctor Hippocrates (Luke, also, was a doctor) regarded a 'young man' in the age bracket 21-28. Another clue is that rabbis began their ministry at about 28-30. According to Luke Jesus began his ministry when he was about 30 (Lk 3:23).

Luke records the young man Saul (Paul) at Stephen's death in a witness-type capacity (Stephen's garments were placed at the feet of Saul), and then quickly has him vigorously persecuting the Christians. This gives a possible age of about 28 for Paul at the stoning of the first Christian martyr (Greek, witness), with an age of early thirties – in the early thirties AD when he was converted. There was a long gap of at least a decade before his first missionary journey from Antioch in Syria, in about 45 AD.

After three years in Arabia (modern Jordan) – the famous escape over the wall from Damascus, and a short period in Jerusalem – Paul went home to Tarsus in Cilicia (south-east Turkey). It was Barnabas who eventually travelled to Tarsus and took Paul to Antioch, which was the third largest city in the Roman Empire. He obviously saw the great potential of this ex-persecutor convert for missionary work in Christ. Luke records Paul teaching for a year 'a large company of people... in Antioch' [where] 'the disciples were for the first time called Christians' (Acts 11:26).

Luke goes on to relate an outbreak of famine, which affected the Christians in Judaea. The church at Antioch, a wealthy cosmopolitan city, decided to send 'famine relief' to their brothers and sisters in the south. The Christian elders sent the aid 'by the hand of Barnabas and Saul' (Acts 11:30). Here was Paul's first involvement in providing financial help for his fellow Christians in need. The famine relief visit to Jerusalem and Judaea was at the instigation of the elders in Antioch. Later, on his second and third missionary journeys, Paul would himself initiate a special collection for the relief of the saints who were poor in Jerusalem.

On completion of his first missionary journey Paul went with Barnabas to Jerusalem to discuss the controversial issue of non-circumcision of Gentile converts. At the end of the discussions Paul tells us in his Galatians letter:

James and Cephas and John, who were reputed to be pillars [of the Church], gave to me and Barnabas the right hand of fellowship...
They would have us remember *the poor*, which very thing I was eager to do (Gal 2:9-10).

During his second stay in Ephesus (third missionary

journey) Paul wrote to the Christians in Corinth reminding them of the contribution for the saints:

As I directed the churches of Galatia, so you are to do. On the first day of the week (Sunday) each of you is to put something aside and store it up, as he may prosper, so that contributions need not be made when I come. And when I arrive, I will send those whom you accredit by letter to carry your gift to Jerusalem. If it seems advisable that I should go also, they will accompany me (1 Cor 16:1-4).

So important was this collection for Paul that he wrote two further letters about it. These letters are now part of our 2 Corinthians, namely chapters 8 and 9. Chapter 8 is written to the city of Corinth; chapter 9 to the province of Achaia in which Corinth lay. In these chapters (letters) Paul 'plays off' one group of churches against the other. There is a kind of healthy spiritual competition!

In chapter 8 (to Corinth) he praises the churches of Macedonia (northern Greece), who had begged Paul for the favour/privilege of letting them join in the relief of the saints in Jerusalem. Out of their poverty they have been generous in giving according to their means. Paul asks the Corinthians to 'give proof, before the churches, of *your* love'.

Writing to the Christians of Achaia (chapter 9) Paul says that he has been boasting about their involvement in the collection to the Christians in Macedonia, stating that their contribution has been ready for a year. He reminded them that 'God loves a cheerful giver', and that their offerings must be given freely, not reluctantly or under compulsion:

You will be enriched in every way for great generosity... for the rendering of this service not only supplies the wants of the saints but also overflows in many thanksgivings to God. Under the test of this service, you will glorify God (2 Cor 9:11-13).

After leaving Ephesus Paul went to Corinth to begin the journey of the collection to Jerusalem. Before leaving Corinth he wrote to the Christians in Rome and informed them about the gift (collection):

At present... I am going to Jerusalem with *aid* for the saints.
For Macedonia and Achaia have been pleased to make some contribution for the poor among the saints at Jerusalem; they were pleased to do it, indeed they are in debt to them, for if the Gentiles have come to share in their spiritual blessings, they (the Gentile converts) ought also to be of service[1] to them in material blessings (Rom 15:25-27).

As Paul was about to sail from Corinth on a pilgrim ship to Jerusalem for the Feast of Passover, a plot to kill him on board was unearthed. He changed plan: back through Greece and over to Troas hoping to arrive in Jerusalem for Pentecost. In Troas he joined the collection delegates from the various churches:

Greece		Asia (Turkey)	
City	*Delegate*	*City*	*Delegate*
Beroea	Sopater	Ephesus	Tychicus
Thessalonica	Secundus		Trophimus
Aristarchus	Derbe	Gaius	
		Lystra	Timothy
			(Acts 20:4-5)

This seems to be a symbolic list based on the symbolic number seven rather than the full delegation. Paul may have represented Corinth since he was the 'founding father' of the Church in that city (1 Cor 3:6), and it is possible that Luke represented Philippi. It also seems odd that Ephesus and Thessalonica have two delegates, and the other cities only one.[2] There is also approximately half-and-half Gentile-Jewish Christian representation: Sopater,

Aristarchus and Timothy were Jewish Christians; the others Gentile Christians.

From Troas Paul sailed to Miletus and there took his leave of the elders of Ephesus. In his famous farewell speech he said:

> I coveted no one's silver or gold...
> You yourselves know that these hands ministered to my necessities, and to those who were with me (Acts 20:33-34).

There may be a hint here of people accusing Paul of not allowing support from the local Christian communities like the other apostles because he had bigger 'money plans', i.e. he intended to abscond with the collection (Paul's opponents used a variety of strategies against him!).

The farewell speech to the Ephesian representatives ended with a mention of 'the weak' and giving:

> In all things I have shown you that by so toiling one must help the weak, remembering the words of the Lord Jesus, how he said: 'It is more blessed to give than to receive' (Acts 20:35).

The only reference to the collection arriving in Jerusalem is in Acts 24 when Paul, under arrest in Caesarea (Palestine), defended himself before governor Felix and the high priest Ananias: 'I came to bring to my nation alms and offerings' (v. 17). Luke hints that Felix knew this referred to the collection for the poor, which may have been a sizeable amount of money: 'Felix... hoped that money would be given him by Paul' (v. 26).

'Paul's pence' (the collection) has been compared to the Jewish temple tax, which every male Jew over twenty had to pay whether they lived in Judaea or other parts of the empire. This tax was delivered three times a year to Jerusalem to arrive for one of the three great feasts – Passover,

Pentecost or Tabernacles.[3] This collection had the protection of the Roman military. Like Paul's collection regular saving was required, and the money was sent to collecting points and accompanied to Jerusalem by delegates. It enabled Jews around the empire to maintain contact and identity with the centre of their faith – the temple.

There was an important difference between Paul's pence and the temple tax:

1. The temple tax had a scriptural basis (Ex 30:11-17); there was no such text for Paul's collection.

2. The Jewish tax was a fixed amount of half a shekel; Paul asked the Christians to give generously according to their means.

3. The tax was a compulsory annual contribution paying for the sacrifices in the temple in Jerusalem; Paul's was a voluntary gift to help the Christians who were poor.

Who were 'the saints who were poor in Jerusalem'? The famous Jewish monastic-type community of Qumran on the shores of the Dead Sea had a 'community of the poor'. Qumran existed from the second century BC to 68 AD and was an 'end time community', i.e. awaiting the coming of the Messiah. The early Christians initially expected the imminent return of Christ (Messiah) so the saints who were poor may have been a special group awaiting in prayer the return of the Messiah to bring in God's final days.

Luke's description of the early Christian community in Jerusalem seems to have the hallmarks of a 'community of the poor':

All who believed were together and had all things in common; and they sold their possessions and goods and distributed them to all, as any had need. And day by day, attending the temple together and breaking bread in their homes, they partook of food with glad and generous hearts, praising God (Acts 2:44-47).

So important was this way of community life in Christ that Luke records it again in chapter 4 verses 32-37.

Barnabas was part of it: he 'sold a field which belonged to him and brought the money and laid it at the apostles' feet' (4:37). We do not know if all the Christians in Jerusalem initially lived like this and then, as numbers increased and expansion began, only a small group kept this particular witness, or whether the poor Christians were a special group from the start.

'Saints' was Paul's normal description in his letter for the Christians – those living a different life-style in Christ from the world around them. The poor Christian group in Jerusalem had given up everything in the steps of Jesus (see complete renunciation theme in Luke 14:25-33), and were giving a special witness to God's cause in Christ (akin to Mother Teresa and her sisters today). As the years passed the poor saints would have needed aid from the wider Christian community. So Paul's pence would have had a practical outcome.

Other more spiritual reasons have been suggested for Paul's collection: fulfilment of Isaiah 66:20: the Gentile nations coming with gifts to Jerusalem for God's making of a new heaven and earth; a gift of gratitude from the Gentile churches for the blessings received from Jerusalem; to promote identification of the Gentile and Jewish converts; a witness to the unity of the Church; a token of the special status of Jerusalem in salvation history; to show Paul's authenticity as an apostle to the Gentiles.

Whatever the reason(s) for this astonishing collection organised by Paul, it stands as a monument as to what one person can do in Christ, which the New Testament record could not ignore.

NOTES

[1] The Greek *leitourgia* is used here, which literally translates as 'liturgy'. The liturgies of Greek city states were financial public services undertaken and promoted by wealthy citizens. This is the spirit Paul asks of the Gentile converts: a public service in keeping with their Greek tradition but in the Spirit of Christ, for Christ in the poor Christians in Jerusalem.

² Luke does not record any specific delegates from Corinth. But in 1 Corinthians 16:1-4 Paul said he would send their accredited delegates with the collection to Jerusalem or they would accompany him.

³ The temple tax was delivered to Jerusalem three times a year:
for Passover   from Palestine
for Pentecost   from lands close to Palestine
for Tabernacles   from distant lands.

11

Paul's apologia

The most famous convert in England in the last century was John Henry Newman. He recorded his spiritual journey in what has been called *the* spiritual classic of the nineteenth century, *Apologia pro Vita Sua*. Newman was steeped in the early Fathers of the Church of whom Augustine of Hippo is the most famous with his spiritual apologia, *The Confessions*. Augustine in turn was influenced by the writings of Paul whose apologia is found in 2 Corinthians, chapters 10-13.

Newman, Augustine and Paul all underwent difficult conversions and were on the receiving end of ill-will or persecution.[1] Their apologias reflect their inward struggles for the God who is Truth and Love at critical times in the life of the Church: Newman amid nineteenth-century agnosticism and rising atheism; Augustine as the Roman empire collapsed before the barbarian invaders; Paul as the Gospel was adapted to the Graeco-Roman empire. Paul's apologia is set in the context of the Church's missionary expansion to the permissive Gentile world with all the dangers this involved inside and outside the Christian community: resistance on the part of the Gentiles; resistance and persecution by the Jews; resistance by strict Jewish Christians who feared a 'sell out' of Jewish Law and traditions; differing interpretations of the Gospel; Christians rallying behind leaders of their own persuasion. It was this last danger which led to rejection of Paul in Corinth for a period of time. It brought a vicious personal attack on Paul by Jewish Christians who sought to reject his claim to be an apostle. Paul's response was his apologia – a letter which revealed what made him 'tick' or, more accurately, who made him tick. The apologia letter (2 Cor 10-13) is, therefore, intensely personal and passionate.

2 Corinthians appears to be an editing of several letters into one long letter. Chapters 8 and 9 have already been treated as letters to Corinth and Achaia in the previous chapter, 'Paul's pence for the poor'. Other possible letters are:

1-2:13	Letter of reconciliation with the Christians in Corinth
2:14-6:13	Letter on the Christian apostolate
10:13	Paul's apologia letter

The apologia is sometimes called 'The letter of tears' because of the agony of mind in which Paul had to write it about 54 AD in Ephesus. It is a stirring and emotional defence of his apostolate/ministry in Christ against those who opposed and undermined him.

Paul, Timothy and Silas were the first Christian missionaries into Corinth: 'We were the first to come all the way to you with the gospel of Christ' (2 Cor 10:14). After a sojourn of eighteen months Paul moved to Ephesus. Then other travelling missionaries like Apollos went to Corinth (Acts 19:1; 2 Cor 11:4). Some of these were strict Jewish Christians (2 Cor 11:22) who regarded Paul as a menace to the God-given Law of Moses. Paul called them false servants of righteousness (2 Cor 11:15). They conducted a vicious anti-Paul campaign in Corinth to discredit him as an apostle.

In the New Testament world the word 'apostle' designated a person sent out on a mission by ship. It was an appropriate word to describe/designate Christian missionaries. The word had a wider application than just The Twelve who were the core apostles. Paul, Barnabas and others were apostles in the broad sense – travelling the

Roman empire preaching and teaching, founding Christian communities and helping to build up already existing communities.

Corinth was a lively charismatic Christian community abounding in the gifts of the Spirit: 'In every way you are enriched in Christ... you are not lacking in any spiritual gift' (1 Cor 1:5-7). But the diversity and abundance of gifts brought its problems, especially when other missionaries came to the city. Groups began to form round particular leaders: 'I belong to Paul... I belong to Apollos... I belong to Cephas...' (1 Cor 1:20). Each group would have had its own orientation: the Pauline group pro-Gentile; the Petrine group pro-Jewish Law and traditions; the Apollos group looking to the intellectual learning of the Graeco-Roman world. 'God's field' (1 Cor 3:5-7; 2 Cor 10:15-16) became ripe for in-fighting and the factious spirit – a disaster for any Christian community.

At some stage during the third missionary journey of Acts, Paul made an emergency visit from Ephesus to Corinth, which is not recorded by Luke. This visit is implied at the end of 2 Corinthians: 'This is the third time I am coming to you' (13:1). It was a distressing visit for Paul because he met severe opposition and humiliation from 'ring leaders'. He had to stay away from Corinth until his reconciling work through Titus and Timothy enabled him to return. It was during this 'stress period' that he sent the letter of tears (apologia) to refute the accusations levelled at him by the 'false apostles' spear-heading the attack against him.

The anti-Paul campaign took the form of a many-sided onslaught. He acts in a worldly way, i.e. he is a deceiver. He plays the humble role when in Corinth but parades boldness when far away in Ephesus (10:1-2). Paul is both crafty and foolish. He does not accept 'income support' when working in Corinth (12:16) but robs other churches by accepting support from them (11:8). This showed that he did not love the Christians in Corinth (11:1). Paul is inferior to the skilled orator apostles (11:5); he's a useless speaker (11:6), has a weak physical appearance, and has to rely on 'weighty letters' (10:10). When at a safe distance he pulls his authority through letters (10:8). As a subtle play on the letters theme the opponents were telling the Christians in Corinth that Paul came to the city with no letters of recommendation. Paul replies:

Do we need... letters of recommendation to you, or from you? You yourselves are our letter of recommendation written on your hearts, to be known and read by all men; and you show that you are a letter from Christ delivered by us, written not with ink but with the Spirit of the living God (2 Cor 3:1-3).

Paul admitted that he was a poor speaker but not lacking in knowledge (11:6). He admitted that he may have boasted a little too much of his authority but this was for building up the Christian community, not to destroy it like his opponents (10:8). He was not trying to frighten them with stern letters. He reminded them that he put into practice what he said and wrote (10:9-11). He allowed the Christians in Philippi to support him but that did not alter the love he had for them – God knows he loves them (11:11).

Paul had no doubts about the threat his opponents meant for Christian community growth in Corinth. Their spirit was wrong, they lacked true understanding of Christ, and were preoccupied with comparing and measuring themselves against each other rather than with Christ (10:12). They were false apostles. Just as Eve was deceived by the serpent so the opponents were 'disguised as apostles' (deceitful workmen) parading as servants of Christ (11:3-4, 13-15). They even take over another missionary's 'field' (Paul's) and boast of what they have done when others have done the planting and watering. They also ignore the need of on-going missionary expansion (10:15-17). Like all cliches they become self-admiration groups. They preach another Christ from Christ crucified and risen as preached by Paul.

Boasting was the 'in-scene' in Corinth. Boasting in the gifts of the Spirit, in whom they owed allegiance too, and the boasting of the super-apostles themselves. In a previous letter Paul had asked: 'Is Christ divided?' (1 Cor 1:13), and follows it with a second question: 'Was Paul crucified?' This was to be the wavelength of his response to the attack, i.e. Christ crucified and risen reflected in the lives of his apostles 'for the word of the cross is folly... but to us who are being saved it is the power of God' (1 Cor 1:18).

Paul also dares to boast (2 Cor 11:21) but it is in the context of the crucified Christ reflected in his ministry which appears as folly to outsiders and even to the super-apostles. This is how Paul can show his opponents in their true colours: they do not focus on the weak and suffering Christ. Paul gives a detailed list of the depths of suffering he has undergone in the cause of the crucified One:

Five times given the thirty-nine lashes in synagogues: this was so severe that people could die. Three times beaten with rods by lictors (attendants of magistrates): this should never have happened because Paul held Roman citizenship; it was a crime to flog a Roman citizen. Once stoned and left for dead (at Lystra – Acts 14:19). Three times shipwrecked (only one recorded in Acts 27) (2 Cor 11:26-25)...

In danger from rivers... robbers... my own people... Gentiles, danger in the city... the wilderness... at sea... danger from false brethren (such as his opponents in Corinth)... many a sleepless night... often without food, in cold and exposure... If I must boast, I will boast of the things that show my weakness (2 Cor 11:26-30).

He had explained in another letter that suffering is of the very nature of being an apostle. The apostolate/ministry involves 'carrying in the body the death of Jesus, so that the life of Jesus may also be manifested in our bodies... So that death is at work in us, but life in you' (2 Cor 4:10-12). Paul's apologia spells out that only those who have suffered personally and in others really know what concern for fellow human beings and their communities requires of us.

From the depths of suffering in Christ Paul turns to the heights of life in the Spirit of Christ. His opponents were boasting about their gifts in the Spirit so Paul boasts of his experience fourteen years previously of being 'caught up to the third heaven'.[2] The third heaven was the heavenly sphere in which the Jews believed Eden was awaiting restoration of the new heaven and earth of God's Day (the Parousia for Christians). It was the sphere of paradise (Persian word for 'garden') which Jesus promised to the good thief (Lk 23:43). When a Persian king wished to honour someone he would give him the right to walk in the royal gardens as the king's companion. This is Paul's imagery of a special experience of being God's companion in Christ (2 Cor 12:1-6).

After the glory came the pain:

To keep me from being too elated...
a thorn was given me in the flesh (12:7).

The Greek word *skolops* can be translated 'thorn' or 'stake'. Impaling people on a stake was turned by the Romans into staking out on a cross. So *skolops* was a word which identified Paul with Christ on the cross. He says that he besought the Lord three times to remove this burden but received the answer: 'My grace is sufficient for you, for my power is made perfect in weakness' (12:9).

It was through the on-going burden of suffering that Paul came to understand the place of suffering in the apostolate:

For the sake of Christ... I am content with weaknesses, insults, hardships, persecutions and calamities; for when I am weak, then I am strong (12:10).

Various interpretations have been given regarding the thorn/stake: spiritual temptations, physical disability, temptations of the flesh, epilepsy, malaria, migraine, eye trouble. The best explanation is the opposition and persecution of his fellow Christians. In the Old Testament 'thorn' refers to enemies. Since Paul is replying to his opponents in Corinth it makes good sense that he refers to them as a thorn in the side. Internal conflict in the Christian communities seemed to agonize Paul (gave him the most suffering) because it hindered community growth in Christ and the spread of the Gospel. But he came to realise that it kept him humble and made him appreciate that it is the Spirit of Christ who must initiate faith and build community in Christ.

Paul intended to visit Corinth again. He hoped that all the quarrelling, jealousy, anger, selfishness, slander, gossip, conceit and disorder would have abated by the time he arrived due to the healing ministry of Titus and Timothy. What a state of affairs had resulted in so gifted a community through faulty teaching and misunderstanding of the true message of Christ!

Paul was prepared to face any charges his opponents might bring against him on arrival but they must be sustained by two or three witnesses. Paul knew the trouble-makers would not easily give up their attack on him. Paul warned them not to be misled by his apparent weakness. Christ was crucified in weakness, but lives by the power of God. 'We are weak in him but in dealing with you we shall live with Christ by the power of God' (13:4).

He informed the Corinthian Christians that he was writing the letter in order that matters might be sorted out before he arrived. He hoped that he would not have to be severe with them in his use of authority given by Christ for the building up of Christian community (13:10).

Meanwhile those opposing him must:
- examine themselves to see whether they are holding on to the faith;
- test themselves;
- mend their ways;
- heed Paul's appeal;

93

— agree with one another and live in peace.

He concluded with a blessing – the best way of making peace with opponents is to pray for them:

The grace of the Lord Jesus Christ
and the love of God
and the fellowship of the Holy Spirit be with you all
(13:14).

NOTES

[1] There were two assassination attempts on Augustine by fellow Christians opposed to his views.

[2] Being caught up into the third heaven may be the same experience recorded as a trance in Paul's speech in Acts 22:17: 'When I had returned to Jerusalem and was praying in the temple I fell into a trance.' This could have been during the period of preaching in Jerusalem some three years after his conversion recorded by Luke in Acts 9:26-30.

12

Pastor Paul (1)

Letters to Titus and Timothy

Three letters in the New Testament are known as 'The Pastorals', i.e. 1 and 2 Timothy and Titus. Eusebius (c. 260-340 AD), Bishop of Caesarea, Palestine, wrote in his famous *History of the Church* that Timothy was the first bishop to be appointed to Ephesus and Titus to the churches of Crete. Tertullian (160-221 AD) said these letters were composed concerning the state of the Church. St Thomas Aquinas in 1274 spoke of 1 and 2 Timothy as concerning Church order and pastoral care. The title 'Pastorals' became fixed in 1726.

All Paul's letters are pastoral in the broad sense of seeking to care for Christian communities ensuring that their faith was rooted into Christ crucified and risen, and that their life-style as communities of faith reflected love, peace and joy. The pastorals show specific concern in the choice of pastors and assistants, their behaviour and administration of the young communities. Like the letter to Philemon they are all written to individuals. They are private letters in contrast to the rest of Paul's letters which are public, i.e. written to church communities.

The pastorals reveal Paul involved in missionary work in places not mentioned in his other letters and Acts of the Apostles, e.g. he had been to Crete and left Titus on the island (Tit 1:5), and he was going to spend the winter in Nicopolis, Western Greece (Tit 3:12). This opens up the possibility that Paul was released from the house arrest recorded at the end of Acts and undertook further missionary work, which is how Eusebius understood events:

'Paul was... conveyed in fetters to Rome...'
Luke... informs us that Paul spent two complete years at Rome (under house arrest)...

Having been brought to trial the apostle set out on the ministry of preaching (Spain?), and having appeared a second time in the same city (Rome) found fulfilment in his martyrdom.[1]

Clement, leader of the Church in Rome, wrote to Corinth about 96 AD and referred to Paul reaching the 'limits of the West', i.e. Pillars of Hercules (Straits of Gibraltar):

Paul... preached in the East and in the West... and after reaching the furthest limits of the West... passed out of this world and was received into the holy places.[2]

Eusebius says that Paul 'in the course of his (second) imprisonment composed the second letter to Timothy.' So it is possible to conjecture a further itinerary of missionary work for Paul after release from house arrest in Rome in about 62 AD. He seems to have gone to Spain as was his intention (Rom 15:28): 'I shall go on by way of you [in Rome] to Spain.' Then to Crete (Tit 1:5), Ephesus (1 Tim 1:3), Macedonia (Greece) from where he wrote to Titus and his first letter to Timothy stating his plan to winter in Nicopolis on the east coast of Greece (Tit 3:12). Then back to the western coast of Turkey reflected in the second letter to Timothy: 'Trophimus I left ill at Miletus' (2 Tim 4:20).

When you come [to Rome] bring the cloak I left with Carpus and Troas, also the books and, above all the parchments (2 Tim 4:13).

The books or papyrus rolls may have contained early forms of the gospels, while the parchments may have been texts of the Old Testament, which were the Scriptures of the early Church. The implication is Paul leaving Troas in haste with no time to collect his cloak, which he would have needed in prison. This suggests arrest. The passage is followed by: 'Alexander the coppersmith did me great harm' (2 Tim 4:14).

Had Paul been to Ephesus again? The harm done by Alexander recalls the riot in Ephesus led by Demetrius the silversmith (Acts 19). Ephesus seems to have been a difficult place for Paul eventually. Luke is strangely reticent about Paul and Ephesus, and does not highlight the strategic missionary importance of this city for Paul in relation to the churches of Greece and the land we call Turkey. This may be due to the serious troubles which befell Paul in the religious capital of this part of the Mediterranean world.

Some big trouble that had occurred in Asia in which Ephesus was situated is reflected in Paul's statement: 'You are aware that all who are in Asia turned away from me' (2 Tim 1:15). There was one exception. Onesiphorus of Ephesus followed Paul to Rome and searched until he found him:

May the Lord grant mercy to the household of Onesiphorus...
he was not ashamed of my chains...
when he arrived in Rome he searched for me eagerly and found me – you well know all the service he rendered at Ephesus (2 Tim 1:16-18).

Paul, who held Roman citizenship, was very conscious of his chains. As he put it: 'wearing fetters like a criminal.' But he turned the situation to advantage: 'the word of God is not fettered' (2 Tim 2:9). Even in prison there was opportunity to evangelise and carry on his pastoral responsibility to young Christian churches.

We do not know much about Titus (Roman name). He was a Greek convert whom Paul and Barnabas took up to Jerusalem at the end of Paul's first missionary journey (Gal 2:1-3). Later he was with Paul in Ephesus, and was sent to Corinth when there was trouble in that Christian community, and it was wise for Paul to stay away (2 Cor 8:16-17). At some stage he was sent, or went with Paul, to Crete to be a model to the Christians on the island (Tit 2:7). He seems to have been a practical man – a good man to send in as peacemaker.

Paul called Titus and Timothy 'true child' (Tit 1:4; 1 Tim 1:2) which suggests they were both converts of Paul. Both are called brother (2 Cor 1:1, 2:13) and fellow worker (2 Cor 8:23; Rom 6:21). Titus is also spoken of as one who walked in the same steps and spirit as Paul (2 Cor 12:18).

The letter to Titus was probably taken by Zenas and Apollos: 'help eagerly on their way Zenas the lawyer and Apollos, and make sure they have everything they need' (3:13). Apollos was the brilliant Christian orator from Alexandria in Egypt who had undertaken a 'preaching tour' of Ephesus and Corinth. Here he was going to Crete with the only Christian lawyer mentioned in the New Testament.

Paul had left Titus in Crete and Timothy in Ephesus with similar tasks to fulfil:

Titus (1:5)	*Timothy* (1:3; 5:17-25)
'Amend what was defective.'	'Charge certain persons not to teach... different doctrine.'
'Appoint elders in every town.'	'Elders... do not be hasty in... laying on of hands.'

Paul reminded them that they shared the same faith, and to avoid false speculation which would undermine the faith (Tit 1:4, 3:9; 1 Tim 1:2-4, 6:20). Titus is told to be uncompromising in teaching the faith (3:8): to give two warnings to false speculators and then shun them (3:9-11). Titus is to follow Paul's example who is 'a slave of God and an apostle of Jesus Christ, to further the faith of God's elect and their knowledge of the truth... through the preaching... entrusted by command of God' (1:1-3).

The letter to Titus and the first to Timothy share two important concerns: (a) advice concerning false teachers undermining the faith of the Christian communities; (b) advice on elders/presbyters in the interests of promoting communities of faith.

False teachers

Titus 1:10-16 deals with false teachers who are 'empty talkers and deceivers, especially the circumcision party (Jewish Christians)... giving heed to Jewish myths... they are upsetting whole families (house-churches) by their teaching...' they must be silenced. These teachers seem to have much in common with the deceivers of 1 Timothy 1:3-7 who are 'desiring to be teachers of the law (Jewish law)... occupying themselves with myths and genealogies which promote speculations rather than a stewardship of God in faith.'

These speculators were probably using the Old Testament genealogies worked up into Jewish myths in the tradition of such works as the second century BC Hebrew Book of Jubilees retelling the story of Genesis and the first part of Exodus with a mixture of fictitious genealogies and legends.

The ancient world was fascinated with origins, and writers loved to tell tales about the beginnings of cities, families and peoples linked with genealogies. This is reflected in the early chapters of Matthew and Luke with their genealogies. Obviously this fascination could get out of hand and end up in naïve speculation as appears to have been happening in Crete and Ephesus – speculation which was side-tracking people from the Christian task in hand: 'stewardship... in faith... the aim of our charge is love... a good conscience and sincere faith (1 Tim 1:5).

The threat from false teachers was not solely from the Jewish side of the Christian communities but from speculations of Greek thinkers influencing Greek Christians. In the second half of the first century AD the beginnings of gnosticism were around – a speculative philosophy which believed the created world was evil and that anything to do with the body was also evil and to be despised. This led to abandonment of marriage and abstaining from food. Speculation of the mind was leading to asceticism and an unhealthy aversion to creation. Paul denounced the speculators as liars with seared consciences and asserted:

> everything created by God is good, and nothing is to be rejected if it is received with thanksgiving; for then it is consecrated by the word of God and prayer (1 Tim 4:4-5).

Elders

It was Paul's custom to appoint elders as soon as a Christian community had been founded (Acts 14:23). So his statement to Titus to appoint elders in every city in Crete implies recent evangelisation of the islands which the Greek poet Homer called 'Crete of the hundred cities'. The Greek word used for 'elders' is *presbuteroi* and is used in 1 Timothy 5:17-19. The background of the presbyters/elders was the Jewish synagogue with its lay elders who were the leaders of the local Jewish communities. They presided over the services in the synagogues and were responsible for discipline in the communities. The rabbis of the synagogue were the commissioned teachers. So it is no surprise to find Paul and his missionary companions establishing communities along similar lines to the synagogues.

Another word is used in Titus and 1 Timothy for community leadership: the Greek word *episcopos* (singular) variously translated as overseer, bishop, presiding elder (Tit 1:7; 1 Tim 3:2). The background here is Graeco-Roman society. The Greeks used *episcopoi* (plural) for appointed regulators of the affairs of a city. The Romans used the word for magistrates appointed to oversee the sale of food in Rome. The word implied oversight and responsibility to higher authority.

In New Testament times elders (*presbuteroi*) and overseers (*episcopoi*) seem to have been synonymous, which is to be expected in Greek-Jewish Christian communities. In Paul's farewell to the Christian leaders of Ephesus at Miletus both terms are used for the same people (Acts 20:17.28). 'Elder' described their liturgical role, and *episcopos* (overseer) their supervisory responsibility over the whole community. By the end of the first century *episcopos* was being used to describe the overseeing of a Christian community in a city – the role of bishop.

In both letters Paul spells out the qualities of the elders (Tit 1:5-9; 1 Tim 3:1-7, 5:17-25); they are to be blameless, even-tempered, gentle, humble, not greedy for gain. They are to be hospitable, lovers of goodness, upright, holy, self-controlled, master of themselves. The letter to Titus emphasises their aptness as teachers (to counteract the false teachers), holding to the faith as taught, instructing in sound doctrine, able to refute contradictors. The elders' qualities in the letter to Titus are based on their stewardship of God.

In 1 Timothy the basis of stewardship is a comparison of managing one's own home and the Church. In the age of house-churches this was obviously very important as was the spirit of hospitality needed in these domestic churches. So elders had to be husbands of one wife, with respectful children, and well-thought of by outsiders. If they oversaw their house-church or circle of house-churches well, preached and taught, they were to receive 'double honour' (double pay). Hence the advice 'no greed for gain'.

Recent converts were not to be made elders. In fact there was to be no haste in laying on of hands (commissioning) for eldership. Members of the community were entitled to rebuke the elders and this was to be done in the presence of all when the community assembled, i.e. the Lord's Day, Sunday (see 1 Cor 5:1-5).

Deacons

1 Timothy 3:8-13 has advice on *diakonoi* (deacons). The passage includes men and women:

Men	*Women*
must be dignified	must be dignified
not double-tongued	not slanderers
not addicted to wine	temperate
not greedy for gain	faithful in all things

The context suggests that both men and women carried out the duties of deacons. In Romans 16:1 Phoebe of Cenchreae is *diakonos* (masculine word). Deacons/deaconesses were assistants to the elders in hospitality, care of community funds, assisting at the Lord's Supper, and distributing welfare to the community. In Acts 6:1-6 seven men were appointed in Jerusalem to undertake welfare work to the Christian community. They were in the tradition of the seven Jewish *parnashin* (welfare workers) in Jerusalem.

The synagogue system from which the initial Christians came had people for dealing with aid to the needy on a community basis. Every Friday two official collectors went round each house collecting donations (money or goods) for the poor and needy. What was collected was distributed to those in need by a committee. This fund for the poor was called the *kuppah* (the basket). It is interesting to note that after feeding the five thousand, Jesus got the Twelve to gather the 'left-overs' into baskets (Jn 6:13) — food taken to the poor?

In addition to the weekly *kuppah* there was a daily fund called the *tamhui* (the tray). This was a collection of food from house to house for those in emergency need for the day. The Christian communities seem to have carried on these charitable tasks which became part of the duties of the deacons.

Widows

These were a particular group who would have needed help. 1 Timothy has a section dealing specifically with them (5:3-16). Distinction is made between 'real widows' (the destitute) and widows who could be cared for by relatives. The community were to assist the destitute widows (5:16), which was the task of the deacons in Jerusalem (Acts 6:1).

For sixty-year old widows, who had been the wife of one husband, there was enrolment into an 'order of widows'. It looks as if this was preceded by a kind of novitiate during which they had to be noted for their good works, their hospitality and washing of the feet at house liturgies, and helping the afflicted (5:9-10). Younger widows were encouraged to remarry (5:14).

Those enrolled in the 'order of widows' had to have brought up children (5:10). This could mean two things. First, that they had brought up their own families in a Christian way. Secondly, it could imply that one of their tasks as widows was 'child rescue'. In the Graeco-Roman world people changed partners with bewildering rapidity. Children became unwanted. It was an age of 'child exposure' (abandonment). If a father refused to accept a child, the child became 'refuse' – thrown out, like rubbish. Unscrupulous people collected them up and 'trained' them for the brothels (girls) and the gladiatorial games (boys). To rescue children from these situations may have been regarded as a Christian duty. What greater love than to give them a Christian home!

These two letters abound in advice to the various groups who made up the Christian communities. Advice to elders, to deacons, to widows, to women in liturgical gatherings (1 Tim 2:9-15), to the rich Christians (1 Tim 6:17-19), to slaves (Tit 2:9-10; 1 Tim 6:1-2), to older men and women (Tit 2:1-5) and younger men and women (Tit 2:6-8). The central wavelength of all advice is Christian goodness reflected in good deeds, which can be summed up in one phrase: 'Be lovers of goodness in faith.'

NOTES

[1] Eusebius, *The History of the Church*, Penguin Classics 1988, p. 97.
[2] The First Letter of Clement to the Corinthians in *Early Christian Writings*, Penguin Classics 1968, p. 26.

13

Pastor Paul (2)

The Second Letter to Timothy

In the first letter to Timothy a number of statements are made which imply Timothy was much younger than Paul:

'Timothy my son' (1 Tim 1:18) ['lad' in one translation]. 'Let no one despise your youth' (1 Tim 4:12),

which implies that some Christians thought him to be too young to be Paul's delegate.

'Do not rebuke an older man, but exhort him as you would a father; treat younger men like brothers' (1 Tim 5:1),

which suggests Timothy may have been mid-thirties in the sixties when the letter was probably written. It can only be conjectured as to how much younger he was than Paul. Luke describes Paul, at the stoning of Stephen in the early thirties AD, *neanias* (young man). The famous Greek Hippocrates, a doctor like Luke, divided human life into seven phases: the fourth phase was 'young man' (21-28). The Jewish reckoning of a young man was similar. Paul must have been about 28 just about to graduate as a rabbi keen to persecute the 'menace' of the Christians.

When Paul first met Timothy at the home of his mother Eunice and grandmother Lois (2 Tim 1:5) Paul would have been in his forties. When Timothy joined Silas and Paul on the second missionary journey about 50 AD, he would have been about fifty. Timothy could have reached maturity as a young man (21), which would give an approximate age difference between Paul and Timothy of some thirty years: Timothy was really like a son to Paul.

Timothy came from Lystra in the province of Galatia (Turkey). Paul and Barnabas evangelised the city on the first missionary journey, and converts included Timothy's grandmother and mother. He was the child of a mixed marriage – his mother was a Jewess, his father a Greek (Acts 16:1). In Greek his name was *Timotheos* made up from two Greek words: *timé* – honour; *theos* – God. So 'Timothy' means 'honour God', which is what he did by becoming Paul's constant missionary companion.

Timothy was with Paul in Troas, Philippi, Thessalonica, Beroea, Athens, Corinth, Ephesus and Jerusalem. He was sent as Paul's special envoy to Thessalonica, Philippi and Corinth for specific pastoral tasks. With Gaius of Derbe he represented the Galatian churches for the collection for the saints who were poor in Jerusalem (Acts 20:4). When Paul wrote from prison to Philippi, Colossae and Philemon the letters were sent in the names of Paul and Timothy. When he was imprisoned for the last time in mid-60s AD, Paul wrote to him in Ephesus and asked him to go to Rome collecting Paul's cloak left behind in Troas (2 Tim 4:21, 31).

The true worth of Timothy to Paul and God's missionary work in Christ is reflected in the letter to Philippi:

I hope... to send Timothy to you...
I have no one like him...
Timothy's worth you know, how as a son with a father he has served me in the gospel (Phil 2:19-22).

Paul wrote from prison in Rome telling Timothy not to be ashamed of 'me, Christ's prisoner, but share in suffering for the gospel in the power of God' (1:8). Paul himself was not ashamed of his imprisonment and sufferings (1:12), which implies that Christians were ashamed of Paul when he was arrested in Ephesus or Troas:

All who were in Asia turned away from me (1:15).

The exception was the household of Onesiphorus:

Onesiphorus... was not ashamed of my chains, but when he arrived in Rome, he searched for me eagerly and found me... you well know all the service he rendered at Ephesus (1:16-18).

The visit to Rome seems to have cost Onesiphorus his life:

May the Lord grant mercy to the household of Onesiphorus for he often refreshed me... may the Lord grant *him* to find mercy from the Lord (1:16-18).

The second letter to Timothy is full of feeling and Paul senses his end has come:

The time of my departure has come (4:6).

He is sensitive about those who have deserted him to the extent of naming some of them – Phygelus, Hermogenes (1:15), and even Demas his fellow worker (Phil v. 24).

Demas, in love with this present world, has deserted me and gone to Thessalonica (4:10).

He refers to Alexander the coppersmith who did him great harm (4:14) and warns Timothy to 'beware of him' (4:15). If this is the same Alexander as mentioned in 1 Timothy 1:20 then it is easy to see why the warning:

By rejecting conscience certain persons have made shipwreck of their faith, among them Hymenaeus and

Alexander, whom I have delivered to Satan (excommunicated) that they may learn not to blaspheme (1 Tim 1:19-20).[1]

It is possible that Christian mischief-makers were turning other Christians away from Paul and were ultimately the cause of his arrest and imprisonment. This is the hardest persecution to endure by one's fellow disciples in Christ, but it is a feature of the lives of the saints down the centuries.

Whatever the mischief Paul was left alone at his preliminary examination:

At my first defence no one took my part; all deserted me. May it not be charged against them (4:16).

Paul forgave like Christ. But he turned the tables and used the situation for evangelisation:

The Lord stood by me and gave me the strength to proclaim the word fully, that all the Gentiles might hear it (4:17).

It would make good sense if this preliminary hearing took place in Ephesus:

All who are in Asia turned away from me (1:15).
At my first defence... all deserted me (4:16).
I was rescued from the lion's mouth (4:17).

In prison in Rome Paul was not completely alone. Luke was with him. Crescens and Titus had been with him but sent to Galatia and Dalmatia respectively. Tychicus had been dispatched to Ephesus presumably with the letter for Timothy (4:10-12).

Paul was also sensitive to the fact that the spread of the Gospel increased opportunities for unsound teaching:

The time is coming when people will not endure sound teaching, but having itching ears they will accumulate for themselves teachers to suit their own likings, and will turn away from listening to the truth... (4:3-4).

Paul's advice to his son in the faith was:

Do the work of an evangelist, fulfil your ministry (4:5)... Be strong in the grace that is in Christ Jesus, and what you have heard from me before many witnesses entrust to faithful men who will be able to teach others also (2:1-2).

He held up the image of the Roman soldier (the one guarding him) as a man of dedication who did not get entangled in civilian pursuits when on service (2:3). The soldier imagery was also used in the first letter to Timothy:

Wage the good warfare, holding faith and a good conscience [as weapons] (1 Tim 1:18-19).

In the circular letter known as Ephesians this soldier imagery is filled out (Eph 6:13-17):

Take the whole armour of God that you may be able to withstand in the evil day and having done all, to stand. Stand[2] therefore, having girded [yourselves] with:

cuirass (loin cover)	of truth
breastplate	of righteousness
sandals	of peace
shield	of faith
helmet	of salvation
sword	of the Spirit

Sensing the end, Paul recalled Timothy's home environment when first they began to co-work in Christ:

You have observed my thinking, my conduct, my aim in life, my faith, my patience, my love, my steadfastness, my persecutions, my sufferings, what befell me at Antioch, at Iconium and at Lystra [Timothy's home city]... all who desire to live a godly life in Christ Jesus will be persecuted... continue in what you have learned and have firmly believed... (3:10-14).

As the letter moves to its climax Paul has a charge:

Preach the word, be urgent in season and out of season, convince, rebuke, exhort, be unfailing in patience and in teaching (4:2).[3]

Then comes a final statement about his own life in Christ:

I have fought the good fight, I have finished the race, I have kept the faith. Henceforth, there is laid up for me the crown of righteousness, which the Lord... will award to me on that Day [Parousia], and not only to me but also to all who have loved his appearing (4:7-8).

Eusebius, in his *History of the Church*, relates Paul being beheaded in Rome in Nero's reign (54-68 AD). He says that Paul was not executed during his first imprisonment (house arrest) in Rome recorded by Luke at the end of Acts: at this stage 'it was easier for Paul's defence of the faith to be received'.[4] But Nero went on to commit abominable crimes. During his second imprisonment in Rome Paul was martyred. Eusebius quotes a letter written by Dionysius of Corinth to Rome:

You have bound together all that has grown from the seed which Peter and Paul sowed in Romans and Corinthians alike. For both of them sowed in our Corinth, and taught us jointly: in Italy too they taught jointly in the same city, and were martyred at the same time.[5]

110

NOTES

[1] In 1 Corinthians 5:1-5 Paul commanded a man living in an immoral relationship with his step-mother to be excommunicated by the community: 'You are to deliver this man to Satan (put out into Satan's sphere of the world) for the destruction of the flesh, that his spirit may be saved in the day of the Lord Jesus' (Parousia). Paul sought the man's salvation and the good of the Christian community by this excommunication.

[2] 'Stand' was the command given to Roman legions in battle. It obliged a soldier to give no ground and to die at his post if need be. The discipline of the Roman armies ensured their ultimate success. No wonder Paul used 'stand' for the spiritual war Christians are engaged in.

[3] A fourth century account states that Timothy was beaten to death by a mob for opposing a heathen festival.

[4] Eusebius, *The History of the Church*, Penguin Classics 1988, p. 99.

[5] *Ibid*. p. 105.

14

Paul and prayer

Many books and articles have been written on Paul's thought particularly regarding justification and righteousness, i.e. how we as sinners get into a right relationship with God. Little has been written on Paul and prayer even though prayer-life is at the heart of a right relationship with God. Prayer is our response inspired by the Spirit to the Father's invitation into relationship, communion and communication with him in Jesus. The circle of prayer begins, continues and reaches its goal with the initiative and aid of God. We even need God's help to opt into the circle of God's love as Paul's 'guide to prayer' indicates in his letters.

In the midst of our hectic life-style akin to the bustling city life of Paul's time we have need to learn about prayer-life from this busiest of Christian missionaries. 'Pray at all times' could well be called Paul's prayer motto.

From the sands of ancient Egypt archaelogists have unearthed thousands of ancient documents including letters. One is from a Roman soldier called Apion to his father Epimachus. The pattern of this personal letter is five-fold:

    (i) Apion sends greetings.
   (ii) He prays that the family is well.
  (iii) He thanks the god Serapis for keeping him safe on the sea voyage.
  (iv) He seeks news from home, and tells his father he soon hopes to be promoted.

(v) Apion greets his brothers and friends, and sends greetings from others with him.

Practically all Paul's letters have this ancient world pattern of letter-writing.

Every letter has an opening greeting:

Paul... to the church of God which is at Corinth.
Paul... to the saints... in Christ at Colossae.
Paul... to Timothy.

Each letter has a 'grace and peace' prayer. 'Grace and peace to you' opens all the letters. Apart from 1 Thessalonians they all add: 'from God our Father'. Excluding Colossians they all have 'and the Lord Jesus Christ'.[1]

It was Paul who used the word 'grace' (Greek: *charis* – gracious gift) most often in the New Testament writings. For Paul grace is an experience – the experience that God loves us despite sin (dis-grace) and comes to us in Christ and his Spirit. Grace is God's free and generous gift of a person (Jesus his Son) who shows us the way to relate to God, and who empowers us to walk and live in the Spirit as he lived.

'Peace' (Greek: *eirene*) is rooted in the Hebrew greeting *Shalom*. We can only be instruments of peace-making if we allow God to work through us in his Son and Spirit. So grace and peace are integrally linked and crucial for any genuine life, and community life, in Christ.

Paul's thanksgiving takes two forms:

1. 'I thank God for you' or
   'I thank God when I remember you in my prayers'
2. 'Blessed be God' (2 Cor; Eph)

Paul was particularly thankful to God for the faith of the Christian communities:

your sincere faith (2 Tim 1:5);
because your faith is proclaimed in all the world (Rom 1:8).

Also for their love:

because... of your love and... faith... towards... Jesus and all the saints (Philem v. 5);
because your faith is growing... love... for one another is increasing (2 Thess 1:3);
because... of your faith in Christ... the love... for all the saints...
the hopes laid up for you in heaven (Col 1:4-5).

With Philippi the thanksgiving reflects the special bond of affection he had with that community perhaps linked with Luke, who may have worked in the retired Roman soldier colony of Philippi:

Thankful for your partnership in the gospel from the first day until now (Phil 1:5).

Paul blessed in thanksgiving God the Father because he had 'blessed us in Christ with every spiritual blessing' (Eph 1:3) and 'comforts us in all our affliction, so that we may be able to comfort those who are in any affliction' (2 Cor 1:4).

There is an insistence on the need for constant prayer in Paul's letters:

Pray at all times;
Pray constantly, give thanks in all circumstances; for this is the will of God in Christ Jesus for you (1 Thess 5:17);
Continue steadfastly in prayer, being watchful in it with thanksgiving (Col 4:2).

If Paul prayed for the Christian communities they are to pray for him and his missionary companions:

Pray for us (1 Thess 5:25);
Pray for us... that God may open to us a door for the word – the Gospel (Col 4:3);
Pray for us that the word of the Lord may speed on and triumph... and that we may be delivered from wicked and evil men (2 Thess 3:1-2);
I know that through your prayers and the help of the Spirit... this will turn out for my deliverance [from prison] (Phil 1:19).

Here we see Paul linking prayer to intentions, which is how he prays:

We always pray for you that our God may make you worthy of his call, and may fulfil every... work of faith by his power (2 Thess 1:11);
It is my prayer that your love may abound more and more, with knowledge and all discernment (Phil 1:9);
I pray that the sharing of your faith may promote the knowledge of all the good that is ours in Christ (Philem v. 6).
We have not ceased to pray for you... to lead a life worthy of the Lord (Col 1:9).

Paul also prayed for the Jews at whose hands he suffered so much:

My heart's desire and prayer to God for them is that they may be saved (Rom 10:1).

The most important insight Paul gives into prayer is that we cannot pray by our own efforts – we need the power (Spirit) of God working within us to pray and guide us in prayer:

God has sent the Spirit of his Son into our hearts crying 'Abba, Father!' (Gal 4:6);

When we cry, 'Abba, Father!', it is the Spirit himself bearing witness with our spirit that we are children of God (Rom 8:15-16).

'Abba' was an address of closeness and intimacy in the Palestine of Jesus and Paul: 'Dad' or 'Daddy' in our culture. It was not used in addressing God in prayer or liturgy where the more formal God, Lord and Father were used. Jesus, as far as we know, was the first person to use 'Abba' in relation to God as Father:

Abba, Father... remove this cup from me (Mk 14:36).

Calling God 'Abba' highlighted the spiritual break-through brought about in Jesus and his disciples. As the Spirit worked through Jesus addressing God as 'Abba' so the Spirit-filled Christians call God 'Abba'. Christians are 'Abba People'. 'Abba, Father' is the wavelength of our prayer-life in the Spirit of Christ. So we should see the Lord's Prayer in this context:

Abba, Father, in heaven
Praised be your name
Your kingdom come
Your will be done on earth as in heaven...

Genuine prayer-life in the Spirit brings the gift of joy as the letter to Philippi states:

In every prayer of mine for you making my prayer with joy (1:4).

This is Paul's prayer experience, and it is to be the experience of Christians:

Rejoice in the Lord always; again I will say, Rejoice... in everything by prayer and supplication with thanksgiving let your requests be made known to God. And the peace of God, which surpasses all understanding, will keep your hearts and minds in Christ Jesus (4:4-7).

With love (Greek: *agape*) joy and peace are central gifts of prayer-life in the Spirit.

In prayer the Lord is at hand. Have no anxiety about anything... I can do all things in him who strengthens me. God is at work in you (Phil 4:6, 13; 2:13).

In Galatians 5:22 Paul expands on prayer-life in the Spirit:

The fruit of the Spirit is love, joy, peace, patience, kindness, goodness, faithfulness, gentleness, self-control.

Love is *the* gift of the Spirit into which all the other gifts of the Spirit in Christian community must be rooted. *Agape* was one of four words in the Graeco-Roman world for love:

eros referred to physical love;
philia to the kind of love we call friendship;
storge to the love and affection between parents and children;
agape was a general word for respect. It was, therefore, the best word into which to pour out all the meaning of God's love at work in Christ.

The importance and significance of agape-love given to us by God through the Spirit of Jesus is seen in its use in key New Testament texts, e.g.:

God is agape	1 Jn 4:8
Love God	
Love neighbour as self	Mt 22:37-38
Love enemies	Lk 6:27

Without agape I am nothing   1 Cor 13:2
Agape is the greatest gift   1 Cor 13:13

The great hymn on Christian love in 1 Corinthians 13 puts agape in perspective in Christian prayer-life:

> If I speak (or pray) in tongues... if I have prophetic powers... understand all mysteries and all knowledge... if I have faith... to remove mountains, but have not love, I am nothing. If I give away all I have... if I deliver my body to be burned [martyrdom] but have not love [agape], I gain nothing (vv. 1-3).

In this hymn composed, or used, by Paul the qualities of agape are spelt out:

Agape is	patient	not	jealous
	kind		boastful
	bears all things		arrogant
	believes in all things		rude
	hopes all things		assertive
	rejoices in right doing	not	in wrong doing
	never ends		irritable
	is the greatest gift		resentful (vv. 4-13)

1 Corinthians 13 is set mid-way between two chapters dealing with gifts-ministries of the Spirit in Christian community. In Corinth there appears to have been a debate about the priority of two gifts concerned with the tongue:

(a) prophecy – interpreting God's will in and for the community;

(b) tongues – a gift not easy to define. It could be described as a spontaneous, abandoned spiritual lilting in the Spirit.

Speaking, praying and singing in tongues is very much of the spirit within Christians, the mind is not to the forefront. The gift of tongues edifies those engaged in this kind of prayer but not one's neighbour. In contrast prophecy speaks to the mind (a prayer of the mind) and edifies the church gathering and potential converts.

The gift of tongues has reappeared in our own times in the charismatic movement. Individuals and communities of people speak, pray and sing in tongues. It was a controversial gift in Corinth as it is today. It needs to be put in perspective in Christian community and individual prayer-life, which is what Paul did across chapters 12-14 of 1 Corinthians. In both lists of gifts-ministries in chapter 12 tongues comes last (vv. 8-11; 27-31). In contrast prophecy is placed after the role of apostle (12:28).

Paul was not against tongues – it is a true gift of the Spirit. He encouraged them to continue with tongues: 'I want you all to speak in tongues' (14:5). Paul himself spoke in tongues more than any of them (14:18). But 'in church', in Christian assembly, Paul's practice was to speak to people's minds rather than in tongues, which people cannot understand, since tongues need interpreting for understanding (14:11.19).

The use of tongues in community gatherings (liturgy) was causing problems (confusion) for possible converts. Outsiders (unbelievers) were mere spectators gaining no enlightenment, which they could 'if all prophesy' (14:24). So Paul advised orderly assemblies (liturgies). Each person with a specific gift-ministry was to have ready:

A hymn (a psalm)
A lesson (some Christian instruction)
A revelation (prophecy by two or three prophets)
A tongue (by two or three speakers in tongues, but only if someone was present who had the gift of interpreting tongues).

References to the variety of liturgical prayer-life in psalms, hymns and spiritual songs are also found in Colossians 3:16, Ephesians 1:13-14, 1 Timothy 2:1-12, 2:8. Paul used psalms, hymns and doxologies from the prayer-liturgy gatherings in his letters:

119

Psalms are quoted frequently across the letter to Rome (3:10-18; 4:7; 8:36; 10:18; 15:9).

Prayers such as:

May the Lord of peace... give you peace at all times in all ways.

The Lord be with you all (2 Thess 3:16; see Gal 1:3-5; Eph 3:14-21).

Blessings like the thanksgiving blessings opening Ephesians and 2 Corinthians. Blessings in the sense of what God bestows on the Christian community for its charitable works such as the collection for the saints who were poor in Jerusalem:

God loves a cheerful giver... And God is able to provide you with every blessing in abundance... You will be enriched in every way for your great generosity... for the rendering of this service (the collection) not only supplies the wants of the saints but also overflows in many thanksgivings to God (2 Cor 9:7-12).

Hymns of which the most famous is 1 Corinthians 13, the hymn on Christian love.

Others comprise:

God's love	Rom 8:31-39
God's mercy and wisdom	Rom 11:33-36
Christ head of all creation	Col 1:15-20
God's plan of salvation	Eph 1:3-14
Christ true God and true man	Phil 2:6-11

Doxology: a combination of Greek *doxa* (glory) and *logos* (word). A prayer/hymn praising and thanking the Father for manifesting his glory through his Word-Son in the power and unity of the Spirit.

Now to him who is able to strengthen you according to my gospel and the preaching of Jesus Christ, according to the revelation of the mystery which was kept secret for long ages but it is now disclosed and through the prophetic writings is made known to all nations, according to the command of the eternal God, to bring about the obedience of faith – to the only wise God be glory for evermore through Jesus Christ. Amen.[2]

NOTES

[1] Apart from Romans a 'grace prayer' ends every letter:
  'Grace be with you' – Pastorals, Colossians, Ephesians.
  'The grace of the Lord Jesus Christ' – all other letters.
[2] *Amen* – 'so be it', in the sense of 'may it continue to be so'.

Appendix 1

Paul: Time Chart

Dates approx AD		Acts of the Apostles	
30	Death of Jesus		
	Stephen martyred. Paul at stoning (a young man)	7:58-60	
	Greek-speaking Christians persecuted	8:1-3	
34(?)	Paul converted	9	
	Preached in Damascus synagogues	9:20	
	3 years in Arabia (modern Jordan)		Gal 1:17
	Return to Damascus		Gal 1:17
37	Escape from Damascus in basket over wall	9:25	
	Preached in Jerusalem	9:26	Gal 1:18
	Sent to Tarsus for his own safety	9:30	Gal 1:21
	Barnabas took Paul to Antioch (Syria)	11:25-26	
	Paul taught for a year in Antioch	11:26	
	Barnabas and Paul to Jerusalem with aid	11:27-30	
45-48	Paul, Barnabas, Mark – First missionary journey	13-14	
48	Paul at meeting in Jerusalem	15	Gal 2:1
50-52	Paul, Silas, Timothy – Second missionary journey	15:36-18:22	
53-58	Paul – Third missionary journey	18:23-26:32	
58-60	Prisoner at Caesarea (Palestine)	23:23-26:32	
60-63	House arrest in Rome	28:30-31	
63-67	Further journeys: Spain (?)		Rom 15:24
	Crete		Tit 1:5
	Greece		Tit 3:12
	Ephesus		1 Tim 1:3
67	Beheaded in Rome under Nero (54-68 AD)		

Appendix 2

Paul: Letters

Missionary Journey	*Date approx.* AD	*Place written*	*Letter/s to*
Second	50-52	Corinth (18 months)	Thessalonica
	52	Ephesus (9 months)	
Third	53-58	Ephesus (30 months)	Corinth
			Philemon (1) Colossae Laodicea Ephesians
	56		Philippi (?) Galatia
	57	Corinth	Rome
	61-63	Rome	Philemon (1) Colossae Laodicea Ephesians
	after 63	Greece	Titus Timothy (1st letter)
	67	Rome	Timothy (2nd letter)

(1) Paul wrote Colossians, Ephesians and Philemon from prison. There is debate as to where he was imprisoned when writing these letters – Rome or Ephesus.

Appendix 3

Missionary Circle of Paul

Travelling companions / co-workers

John Mark	Acts 13:13; Col 4:10-11; Philem 24
Barnabas of Cyprus	Acts 13:2; Col 4:10-11; Gal 2:1
Timothy of Lystra	Acts 16:3; Rom 16:1
Titus	Gal 2:1; Tit 1:5; 2 Cor 8:23
Silas (Silvanus)	Acts 15:40; 1 Thess 1:1; 2 Thess 1:1
Luke	Col 4:14; Philem 24
Aristarchus of Thessalonica	Acts 20:4; 27:2; Philem 24; Col 4:10

Named co-workers

Philippi	Epaphroditus (fellow soldier)	Phil 2:25
	Euodia	Phil 4:2
	Syntyche	Phil 4:2
	Clement	Phil 4:3
Corinth	Phoebe (deaconess)	Rom 16:1
	Aquila & Priscilla	Acts 18:3
Ephesus	Onesiphorus	2 Tim 1:15-18
Colossae	Philemon	Philem 1
	Archippus (fellow soldier)	Philem 2; Col 4:17
	Tychicus	Col 4:7; Eph 6:21
	Epaphas	Col 1:7; 4:12-13; Philem 23
	Jesus called Justus	Col 4:10-11
	Demas (who later deserted)	Col 4:14; Philem 24; 2 Tim 4:10
	Mary	Rom 16:6
	Persis	Rom 16:12
	Tryphaena ⎱ twin	Rom 16:12
	Tryphosa ⎰ sisters (?)	Rom 16:12
	Urbanus	Rom 16:9
	Andronicus ⎱ husband	Rom 16:7
	Junias ⎰ & wife (?)	Rom 16:7

All the twenty-four people greeted in Romans 16 would be workers in the Lord, six of whom were women.

Scribes for Paul:

Tertius	Rom 16:22
Silas (Silvanus)	1 & 2 Thess 1:1; cf 1 Pet 5:12
Sosthenes	1 Cor 1:1

Letter bearers:

Pheobe	Romans
Tychicus	Colossians, Ephesians, Philemon
Titus & Timothy	Letters to Corinth
Epaphroditus	Philippians
Timothy	Letters to Thessalonica
Zenas – Apollos	Letter to Titus

Appendix 4

Paul: Christian communities

	Turkey	Greece	
Founded by Paul	Antioch (Pisidia) Lystra Iconium Derbe	Philippi Thessalonica Beroea Athens Corinth	Spain (?) Malta (?) Crete (?)
Worked in	Jerusalem Damascus Antioch (Syria) Cyprus (Crete) Perga (Pamphylia) Troas Ephesus Rome	Arabia (?) Tarsus (?) Spain (?)	
Visited	Miletus Tyre ⎤ Palestine Ptolemais ⎬ coast Caesarea ⎦ Acts 21:4-8		

These are the places we know about. There must have been many others acros Paul's thirty-three years as missionary pastor.

Jerusalem   Headquarters of the early Church until about 66 AD when Christians left due to the Zealot uprising, and went to Pella.

Antioch (Syria)   Paul's missionary base.

Ephesus   Strategic centre for Paul in relation to churches he founded in Greece and Turkey.